GOODBYE TO PITH HELMETS

Sir Alan Burns meeting Chiefs at a Durbar in Kumasi

Canham Collection published by kind permission of Cambridge University Library

Goodbye to Pith Helmets

A District Commissioner's account of the
last years before Ghana's Independence

PHILIP DENNIS

The Pentland Press
Edinburgh – Cambridge – Durham – USA

© Philip Dennis, 2000

First published in 2000 by
The Pentland Press Ltd
1 Hutton Close
South Church
Bishop Auckland
Durham

The illustrations marked Canham Collection are published
by kind permission of Cambridge University Library, which
holds the originals as part of the former Royal
Commonwealth Society Library.

ISBN 1-85821-789-X

Typeset in AdobeGaramond 11/13
by Carnegie Publishing
Carnegie House
Chatsworth Road
Lancaster
Printed and bound by Bookcraft (Bath) Ltd

Contents

Introduction and Acknowledgements   1

Chapter   *Page*

    I   When the Wind Changed   5

   II   Colonial Service Began on the Beaches   12

  III   The Army Brings West African Unity   26

  IV   Sierra Leone   38

   V   The Economic War   53

  VI   Sekondi-Takoradi   65

 VII   The Burns Reforms   79

VIII   Sir Gerald Creasy's Inheritance   99

  IX   Togoland   105

   X   Ewes Outside Togoland   124

  XI   Sir Charles Arden-Clarke   136

 XII   The Final Phase Begins   148

XIII   Independence Approaches   165

XIV   Turmoil on the Way to Independence   179

XV   Reflections in Retrospect   196

Appendix

   I   Historical Events Before 1939   205

  II   Bibliography   209

     Index   211

Introduction and Acknowledgements

My first acknowledgement must be to Faith, my wife, for her help in this work, but especially for providing me with a title. I thought of the title 'Ghana Led the Way' as indeed it did amongst African colonies achieving independence. However, I think the title now chosen is better for a book about the latter days of colonial rule, as the pith helmet was an important symbol. When I first went to Africa it was regarded as essential to keep off the sun and when I left it was still part of the ceremonial colonial uniform.

My purpose in writing the book has been to portray the last years of colonial rule in the Gold Coast, as I saw them from a District Administration point of view, and relate this to political developments. In so doing I have tried to give a fair account of the part of some of my friends and colleagues. I have also thought it of interest to mention in some cases how different people adapted themselves after colonial service to various roles. I hope I have given the impression that redundancy is not necessarily such a disaster as it is sometimes thought to be. We experienced redundancy and the situation was handled well by the Colonial Office; this does not always happen in the case of all employers. The cheerful approach of colleagues to the end of colonial service is I hope conveyed in some of the anecdotes related; and here I must also pay a tribute to my Ghanaian friends and colleagues who showed great understanding of the position of expatriates and at the same time helped us to approach the situation in the country with understanding.

In an appendix there is a list of books which I have consulted both during my colonial career and later. Some were only written later but these have been especially helpful. In writing about books I must make a special mention of the Library of the Royal Commonwealth Society and also Terry Barringer. She was the last of the six librarians since the Society was founded in 1868 with the special intention of setting up a

I

library. Terry has helped me with suggestions regarding the form and text of the book and in providing encouragement towards writing it at all. Regarding the library I can only write with some degree of relief as it nearly became lost altogether as a collection of books and other items connected with Commonwealth countries. When the Society had to close its doors at the end of 1991 owing to financial difficulties the library was valued at £3 million and had to be used as an asset together with the freehold building. Through great efforts by the staff and others the library was kept going and sold to a Trust which gave it to Cambridge University. It was fortunate that Terry Barringer was able to continue as librarian, but now only on a part-time basis, as the University does not feel able to fund a full time post. It is with some sadness that I have to comment that the Royal Commonwealth Society now re-opened as a club has at the time of writing not thought fit to provide any funds for the library which was a primary purpose for its foundation.

In writing this book I have also received help from Rhodes House in Oxford and the map room of the Royal Geographical Society. I am also indebted to Rodney Bennett for supplying me with some papers illustrating the great humour of Robin Blair, who is mentioned later in the book. Lastly, but by no means least, I must thank Joy Wallbank for her transformation work through her word processor. It has been a great pleasure to work with her.

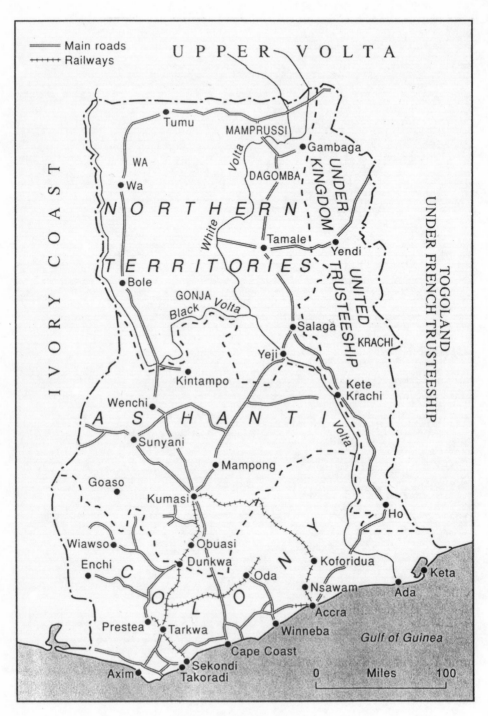

The Gold Coast *c.*1950.
Reproduced with permission of the Controller of Her Majesty's Stationery Office

4

CHAPTER I

When the Wind Changed

THE NORMAL TRANQUILLITY of Accra on a Saturday afternoon was shattered in February, 1948, by several rifle shots. These were fired by the police to halt a march by ex-servicemen. The march was stopped, but rioting broke out in the town and elsewhere. At the time nobody could have known that the 28th February, 1948, would mark the beginning of a movement to end colonial rule throughout Africa. It is, however, now clear that the beginning was in Accra capital of the British colony of the Gold Coast.

Tragically an ex-sergeant Adjitey was killed and another man died later. Adjitey was in the forefront of the march intending to take a petition to Government House at Christiansborg Castle. Permission had been granted to the marchers to deliver their petition at the Secretariat in a different part of Accra. They had already overwhelmed a line of police attempting to keep them on their authorized route. The British Superintendent of Police in charge at the crossroads near Government House tried to stop the march with tear gas, but unfortunately the canisters did not function. The Superintendent, Colin Imray, was an experienced officer with service in Palestine, and his action was vindicated by the Commission set up under Aitken Watson KC to enquire into the rioting.

Compared with happenings in British India the shooting in Accra was of a minor nature. Shooting by police in the Gold Coast was, however, very rare indeed. Rioting was more commonplace, but it was usually connected with local matters, such as a stool dispute concerning the deposition of a chief from his stool (the local equivalent of a throne), or a land dispute. On this occasion the rioting was directly opposed to the colonial government. Apart from the grievances of ex-servicemen over the lack of employment, which they felt they had been promised, there was general dissatisfaction in the country; the farmers thought the price of cocoa should be higher, whilst in the towns there were shortages of many commodities and price control was ineffective. Large overseas companies bore the brunt of the blame for shortages and resulting high prices, at least in the minds of the public. In fact of course the Gold Coast was suffering from a world-wide problem after the end of World War II in 1945.

In Accra looting, arson and general rioting continued until rain fell in the evening and there was little left to loot from the shops. Then lorry loads of hopeful looters travelled to other towns such as Nsawam, Akuse and Koforidua. These towns had been denuded of most of their police in order to reinforce the police in Accra. Looters on the way to Koforidua, for example, could thus have passed police going in the opposite direction. In Koforidua an Inspector of Police achieved many convictions in the courts some months later through simply watching from a distance and taking notes. The District Commissioner in Akuse, Jimmy Chalmers, tried direct intervention, which worked for most riots, but on this occasion a brick was thrown through his car windscreen and he had to retire hurt.

Sporadic rioting continued for about a month largely in towns outside Accra, including Kumasi, the capital of the state of Ashanti. Political leaders, who tried to use the rioting as a reason for demanding the hand-over of power by the colonial government, were arrested and detained at different centres in the north of the country. The six detainees included Dr J. B. Danquah, leader of the United Gold Coast Convention, and Kwame Nkrumah, who subsequently became the first Prime Minister and later President. All the persons detained were released by the time the Watson Commission started its hearings.

The Watson Commission found that the riots were organized, but it was unable to say how or by whom they were organized. It is doubtful whether there was a recognizable organization. A spontaneity common in Africa and associated with a number of events seems more likely. The local politicians made use of the events spurred on by the recent independence gained by India, Pakistan and Ceylon. The Watson Commission went a long way towards encouraging them by recommending a new constitution to run for a trial period of ten years. In fact independence was gained in nine years after a series of constitutional changes. It is interesting to note that India and Pakistan became independent some ninety years after the Indian Mutiny of 1857; the Mutiny was a much more sanguinary affair than the Gold Coast riots.

There was much surprise in Accra at the intensity of the rioting, but in the district administration to which the writer belonged it was well known that there were many potential sources of trouble. Some six months before the riots I was told by a very senior officer in the Secretariat that the resettlement of ex-servicemen had gone very smoothly. When I said that this was not my experience I was met with silence and incredulity.

The famous 'Wind of Change' speech made by Mr Harold Macmillan (later Lord Stockton) did not come until several years after Ghana's independence, but the wind could be said to have changed in Accra in February, 1948. The history of Africa would not have been greatly different if the rioting in Accra had not happened, but it was a turning point worth historical recording. There are a number of different interpretations of colonial history in Africa. It can be represented as an era of greedy exploitation, or at the other end of the scale as a period of enlightened progress. The truth lies somewhere between the two, but it is wrong to regard present day happenings in Africa as a legacy of colonial times. There could be an argument for saying that the British and other European nations were irresponsible in letting go of their powers as quickly as they did. Greater delay was, however, hardly a practical proposition and much good-will would have been lost.

This book is about the years between 1939 when World War II began and 1957 when Ghana achieved independence. For nearly the whole of that period I served either in the Gold Coast, as Ghana was then called, in the Colonial Administrative Service, or in the Army elsewhere in West Africa. I shall try to relate personal experiences to what was happening in the Gold Coast, and in the world at large, where World War II was the main influence on events. In my work in the Administration I was in day to day contact with Ghanaians of many occupations from lawyers and doctors to road labourers and also with both British and Ghanaian service colleagues.

An outline of the historical background to the Gold Coast before the period between 1939 and 1957 is given in Appendix I. In the meantime it suffices to say that the Portuguese were the first Europeans to set foot in Ghana at Elmina in 1469. They built a castle there which was captured by the Dutch in 1637. The map of forts and castles illustrates how various nations established trading posts along the Gold Coast. For the most part the development was carried out by Chartered Companies or similar organizations. The interest was mostly in trade, although there was much dedicated missionary activity. The original incentive to the Portuguese was to find gold, as the capture of Ceuta on the Mediterranean coast led them to believe quite rightly that there was a source of gold in West Africa. Thereafter the slave trade developed. First of all it was simply a matter of taking a few slaves home to Portugal, but later the Portuguese and other European nations developed a trade in conveying slaves across the Atlantic to newly established colonies. There were no strong moves against this brutal trade until the end of the eighteenth century. These moves led in Britain to the Wilberforce Act of abolition of 1807 and thereafter a British ascendency in the Gold Coast was gradually established. Britain can at least claim to have been at the forefront of moves to abolish slavery, but towards the end of the nineteenth century Britain was also a major player in the scramble for Africa. This was an uninspiring rush to annexe territory for commercial exploitation. Frontiers were established with little regard to ethnic considerations and these frontiers largely persist today.

The final act in the case of the Gold Coast frontiers (now those of Ghana) came with the defeat of Germany in World War I and the division of Togoland between Britain and France.

Sketch map by
Ted Hatch of the
Royal Geographical
Society

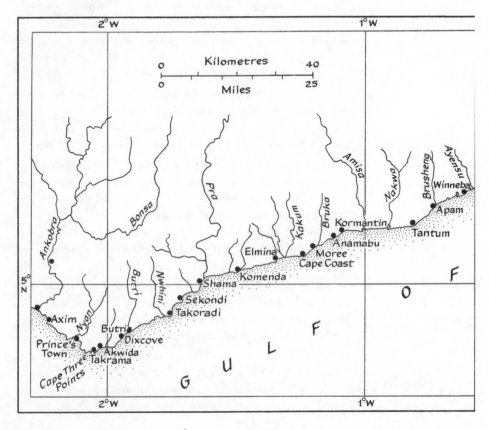

The additional territory was consigned to Britain and France under League of Nations Mandate and later came under United Nations Trusteeship. This additional territory brought the total area of the Gold Coast and present day Ghana to 91,985 square miles, which is just slightly smaller than the United Kingdom of Great Britain and Northern Ireland. The country is roughly rectangular in shape varying between 200 and 250 miles from east to west and with an average distance of about 400 miles from the northern boundary to the coast. The land is mostly well below 1000 feet in height apart from rising to 3000 feet in part of Togoland; there are also hills around Tarkwa and scarps north of the Accra plains and around Mampong in Ashanti. The main change in landscape is between fairly open country in a coastal belt running east and west from Accra, forest in the central part of the country and a more open savannah landscape in the north. Accra is just west of the Greenwich meridian and just south of latitude 6°N. The climate is tropical with temperatures of over 80°F for most of the year, and a monsoon type of rainfall. This mostly falls between March

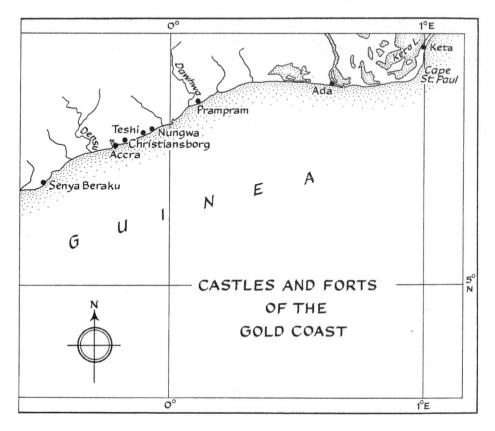

CASTLES AND FORTS
OF THE
GOLD COAST

and November and varies in amount from around 30 inches per annum in Accra to nearly 80 inches in Axim. The rainy season is shorter in the North and the dry season is affected by the Harmattan, a dry wind off the Sahara, which brings cooler nights. The high humidity associated with daytime temperatures of around 80°F and a little higher has an enervating effect on health particularly for Europeans. The main cause of ill health, however, particularly in the nineteenth and early twentieth centuries, was from malaria and other mosquito-borne diseases. Poor sanitation also caused enteric diseases and tsetse flies spread trypanosomiasis (sleeping sickness) amongst humans, cattle and horses.

Elmina Castle

When I first went to the Gold Coast, political progress was seen as something to be achieved through the development of African institutions, with self government or dominion status as a very long-term objective. This had to change. There was a continuance of the functions of maintaining law and order and developing education, agriculture, health services, forestry and communications of all kinds; the difference was that we did not know for how long we would be doing these things. There was the same sense of trusteeship developed earlier, but it became difficult to know for whom we were trustees. I think most administrative officers regarded our duties as mainly for

Cape Coast Castle
from the shore

the benefit of the ordinary citizens in their towns and villages; we thought they required protection from unfair commercial exploitation and oppressive rule by their chiefs and elders. A seemingly insoluble problem was how far we should give protection from nationalistic politicians using their countrymen for their own ends. Like many politicians elsewhere in the world they could be seen to have a priority of interest in their own advancement.

It could have all been very dreary work, but we were greatly helped by a natural rapport with Ghanaians. It was almost impossible to take life too seriously with such cheerful people around. At times we were guilty of laughing at Ghanaian ways, and they certainly had their share of humour at some of our antics. For most of the time, however, we laughed together and laughter played a great part in making a peaceful solution to many problems; there was great goodwill on both sides. There will be many seeming trivialities in this book, but I hope they will give some indication of a cheerful and happy life by no means weighed down by difficulties inevitable in the latter years of a colonial regime.

CHAPTER II

Colonial Service Began on the Beaches

HITLER'S INVASION of The Netherlands, Belgium and Luxembourg began on the 10th May, 1940. On the same day fourteen cadets for the Colonial Administrative Service, including the writer, arrived off Accra in the oldest Elder Dempster passenger ship, the *Ada*. Much of the journey had been in convoy, but the Gulf of Guinea was still regarded as safe from submarines, so we anchored off Accra and landed by surf boat. We were all dressed in lightweight suits and topees, although this was hardly suitable for a landing on a beach with powerful breakers, or for a hot Customs shed. Most landings on the Gold Coast before Takoradi Harbour was opened in 1928 had been on beaches and the custom was continued for administrative cadets. Arrival in Accra made it possible for them to be interviewed in the Secretariat; here there was presumably a judgement made on our suitability for different parts of the country. There had of course already been a selection by the Colonial Office for different parts of the Empire and some description of the selection process and how the writer found himself on the beach will now be given.

At the recruitment stage the Colonial Service was a unified one and this applied not only to the Administrative Service, but to Departments such as Police, Education, Agriculture and Forestry. For the Administrative Service recruitment was mainly conducted amongst university students in their final year before graduation. There was a tendency for a preponderance to come from the universities of Oxford and Cambridge. The main reason for this was a lack of publicity for the service in some other universities. The Colonial Office had plenty of candidates for relatively few jobs and was content to deal mainly with the Appointment Boards of Oxford and Cambridge. The selection process consisted of interviews first by members of the Appointments Board, later by a Colonial Office official, and a final selection board composed of colonial gentlemen with service in the UK and overseas. The last seemed elderly and formidable at the time, but in fact they should be described as middle-aged and helpful. One candidate, when asked where he wanted, to go named Nigeria as his favoured country, but had to go to consult a map immediately afterwards to find its location. He was one of the few candidates sent where he asked to go.

Regarding the Colonial Office, which was spread out around London, I remember going to Queen Anne's Gate to be interviewed. An attempt was made to persuade me to write down the Police as an alternative to the Administrative Service in view of my military interests as a member of the University O. T. C. and the Air Squadron. I avoided doing this as I was not interested in being a policeman; it was only much later I found out that the pay was lower.

It is probably fair to say that pay was not a major consideration amongst undergraduates of the nineteen thirties when considering careers. More important was finding an interesting career with reasonable security of employment. Amongst those who applied for the Colonial Service there was perhaps a wish to avoid a humdrum life and an interest in countries and peoples outside Britain. Information about the Colonial Service came to different people in a variety of ways. Some had relatives in different forms of public service; in my case my father was a regular army officer. I had carefully considered this as a career,

A busy scene with fish being brought ashore

but I did not want to go straight from school to an army career, which at the time was the normal procedure. I preferred to go to a university, so I took a degree in Geography at Oxford. My father was serving in Gibraltar at the time and I obtained some ideas on the Colonial Service from there. I still had the option of going into the army from Oxford, but as an undergraduate of the nineteen thirties I was part of a somewhat confused generation. If war came, as seemed likely, we should virtually all have to join the armed services. Many undergraduates had distinctly pacifist views; some of these later distinguished themselves in the armed services. In general there was a great distaste for fighting people whether they were German, Italian or of any other nationality. There was more overseas travel than amongst previous generations and more internationally minded feelings. Amongst those joining the Colonial Service there was a general belief in the British Empire as something of value as a civilizing influence, but we were not particularly enamoured of Kipling and what appeared to us as a 'rose coloured spectacles' approach. We laughed heartily at David Lowe and his Colonel Blimp cartoons in the Evening Standard. At the same time there was a feeling of wanting to do something positive and useful for Britain.

The process of selection for the service in 1939 was carried on under the cloud of impending war. Neville Chamberlain's ill-named policy of appeasement had obviously failed. His final attempt in 1938 at Munich at preventing war was, however, generally welcomed amongst young people, and he should be given credit for the time gained for preparation. Selection for the Colonial Service continued largely without taking account of the prospect of war. Sir Ralph Furse was the driving force behind the process in the nineteen thirties and he was working in this role at the time the war started for Britain on the 3rd September 1939. He was one of the persons responsible for seeing that those selected in August went into training and on to overseas postings. There was some confusion, particularly for persons like the writer who also had some commitment to the armed services, but by the end of September there was a clear direction that anyone who joined the forces should do so in the colony to which he had been posted.

In October a course known as the Tropical African Services (T. A. S. for short) Course began at both Oxford and Cambridge. It normally lasted a year, but on this occasion was reduced for the Gold Coast to two terms. It was a well designed course from the point of view of imparting information about a wide range of subjects in a short time; it did not attempt to give much information about the daily work of an administrative officer. The law section of the course particularly impressed me and led me some years later to qualify as a barrister at the Inner Temple. I had hitherto regarded the law as something which happened in dull and dusty solicitors' offices; such eminent academic lawyers as Stallybrass and Fifoot quickly dispelled this view. We spent a morning in the Oxford Magistrates Court which was unfortunately largely concerned with offences against the blackout regulations. The fine was five shillings (25p) for nearly everyone who pleaded guilty, but one person who pleaded not guilty was fined ten shillings (50p). This struck me as most unjust at the time, but in later years sitting as a magistrate in Africa there seemed to be much more logic in it.

Our reactions as course members to different lectures on Africa were to some extent indicative of our attitudes to Africa and Africans. We regarded Professor Coupland who lectured on the British Empire as somewhat 'Blimpish', although we learnt later that when this got back to him he was surprised as he regarded his views as a little socialistic. We did not appreciate points made by Dr Fortes (later Professor Fortes) who lectured as a social anthropologist. He had done research work in Africa including some amongst the Frafras of the Gold Coast and he tried to get us to understand that for them and other Africans spending the night dancing could be more important than getting their crops planted; our practically based minds regarded this as a negative attitude. Much later this was put to me in more terse terms by Sir Thorlief Mangin as a Chief Commissioner. He said that we had to learn 'to think black'. The word 'black' was not used in any derogatory sense, but to express the need to see things as Africans saw them. It is a theme that will be considered later, as it was something which we often failed to do.

Another lecturer worthy of note was Margery Perham, who had spent some years studying colonial rule in Africa. She outlined the principles of indirect rule as developed by Lord Lugard in Northern Nigeria early in the century; Lugard was responsible for the extension of British rule from the south to the Emirates of the north. Here the development of indirect rule through authoritarian chiefs was a practical way of resolving the problem of gaining administrative control. Margery Perham had a high regard for Lord Lugard, whom she knew personally; he was undoubtedly an able soldier and administrator, but whether a system designed for a certain set of circumstances should have been adopted as a general philosophy is more doubtful. The states of the southern half of the Gold Coast amongst others operated on different principles. Margery Perham was a persuasive lecturer and writer, but her theories were not necessarily for general application.

A somewhat alarming series of lectures concerned health and hygiene in the tropics. There was a weekly dose of diseases and precautions to take. There were pictures too including some of the effect of elephantiasis – a mosquito-borne disease with enlarging effects on the male genital organs. The only comfort after we had seen the pictures was a remark that it takes a long time to get as bad as that.

The language training was probably the least useful from the Gold Coast point of view. We were all taught Twi, which only covers Ashanti and a part of the rest of the country adjacent to it; it was spoken in about one third of the whole country. It is a tonal language and can only be learnt properly by daily use. However, we all learnt something from our contact with Akufo Addo, a Twi speaking barrister living in London at the time. He had political views which were apparent although he refrained from thrusting them at us; these later resulted in his being detained with five others after the riots in Accra in 1948. In the years after independence he received his deserved reward in being made a High Court judge. In the intervening years he had succeeded in making his profession his main consideration; he did not really want to be in conflict with the British.

At the end of the course there was an examination and a final interview with a board at the Colonial Office before we were told whether we had passed. At my interview I was asked a question about forced labour, as one of my answers had suggested that there might be some forms of coercion such as having to earn money to pay taxes. However, I readily agreed that there was no forced labour in British colonies and I was allowed to go. I left chuckling to myself as the interview reminded me so much of one depicted in the Douglas Fairbanks (Jnr) film *The Sun Never Sets* about the British Empire. In this film a candidate was asked 'What would you do if you were bitten by a mad dog in the desert many miles from any medical aid?' After some thought the candidate said 'Die, Sir.' 'Quite right' came the reply and he was sent on his way with the general approval of the board.

There has been a digression from arrival on the beach at Accra, but it perhaps gives some indication of how the selection and training of cadets (as we were called) brought together people with a generally similar background and outlook. It may give some clue to Colonial Office philosophy on the colonies in the inter-war years, but this was quite difficult to discern at the time. In general economic developments were deemed to be good whilst political developments were not encouraged unless they followed traditional forms. Much was left to individual governors who as in the case of Gordon Guggisberg of the Gold Coast left his mark in economic development; he was fortunate in governing a colony which was relatively well off financially. British politicians of all parties were necessarily much concerned with India where there was a strong political movement engendered by Mahatma Gandhi. The African colonies, however, attracted little attention in being apparently trouble free.

After a night in Accra staying with Mr Mangin (later Sir Thorlief) sharing a guest room with another cadet, John Deakin, I set off for Cape Coast. I was accompanied on the front seat of the lorry by John Spicer, a friend of mine on the course and a cabin mate on the sea journey. He was going to Tarkwa further on and in the Western Province, whereas Cape Coast was in the Central Province. I only saw John once again for a few minutes, as he joined the RAF and was sadly posted 'missing' and subsequently presumed killed in the Middle East. The lorry journey was memorable for the insistence of the driver that he was saving petrol by coasting downhill and coming almost to a standstill before re-starting with a great spluttering of the engine and a grinding of gears.

At Cape Coast I was the junior of two Assistant District Commissioners under Gough Mackay, who was in turn under the Provincial Commissioner, Mr A. F. E. Fieldgate. We all worked in an old building largely of wooden construction on stilts similar to many put up by the British early in the century. There were two storeys with the Provincial Commissioner fittingly on the top. Lionel Gardner was the Assistant DC. He

had arrived in the country some eight months previously and was in charge of my inauguration. My first job was taking over from him as officer in charge of prisons.

The Main Street in Cape Coast Town Centre

The prison in Cape Coast was situated in the old castle where slaves had been held before shipment across the Atlantic. The accommodation was improved since those times and going to prison was not regarded as a particularly awe-inspiring fate. The stone walls retained the heat, although the whole building was cooled by sea breezes. The top floor housed the post office.

The Prison Department was under a Director who was stationed in Accra and was responsible for all the prisons in the Gold Coast; each one of them had a Keeper of Prisons (KOP), who came under the Director. At each location the officer in charge on the spot was the District Commissioner, or whoever he appointed. The duties of the officer in charge were not very clearly defined, but he was responsible for matters needing local attention including disciplinary offences by prisoners. As well as the Cape Coast prison there was a prison for lepers housed in Fort St Jago at Elmina. There was not much

Cape Coast Castle

for the officer in charge to do in either case, but the Elmina prison seemed to me to need more supervision in that lepers as imprisoned outcasts of society required some consideration.

There was a custom amongst KOPs when reporting to the DC or officer in charge to salute and say 'All correct, Sir'. At first I thought this was intended as a reassurance that all was well. I learnt quite soon that it was simply a custom and some years later I was given the delightful report 'All correct, Sir. One prisoner escaped'. This was a very unusual occurrence, although there was ample opportunity to escape when prisoners were out in a labour gang with one warder for about eight or nine prisoners. In 1940 they carried out much useful work around the town and government residential areas, but this had to be curtailed later owing to various international labour conventions. The larger prisons gave trade training and I have seen an advertisement by a shoemaker reading 'trained in HM Prisons'. I had no fear about losing my shoes, as his time in prison had turned him into a useful citizen.

It is perhaps anomalous to describe the relationship of a DC with other departments by starting with the Prisons Department. At the same time the relationship with this department was closely connected with responsibilities for law and order. Prisons represented a translation of a European system to West

Africa, but amongst the local people, there was greater interest in restitution to persons aggrieved than in punishment of the offender.

Relations with the police were more important from the point of view of law and order. In this respect the duties of a DC were not very clearly defined, but any powers there were stemmed from his position as a magistrate, whilst there was a general duty of being responsible for good government in his district where he was the Governor's representative; there was of course a chain of command through Chief Commissioners and Provincial Commissioners. The Police had a similar chain of command from a Commissioner of Police to whom they were all responsible. This apparent dichotomy might have been expected to lead to problems, but in practice these were few.

There were two categories of policemen, namely General Police and Escort Police. The former covered all police duties, and could through promotion advance to the higher ranks in the service, whilst Escort Police were a wholly African force under the overall command of the General Police; they were responsible for patrol work, crime prevention, crowd control and as the name suggests for escorting bullion or valuable goods around the country; they were often ex-servicemen and wore a military style of uniform. The Escort Police were certainly a deterrent to wrong-doers when they came on the scene. In 1940 nearly all the ranks of the police above that of Inspector were held by British officers, but the process of promotion of Africans to senior posts took place over a period of years.

Relationships between the DC and heads of departments such as Agriculture, Forestry, Education, Medical and Public Works normally worked well in a loosely defined way. A management lesson quickly learnt by a junior administrative officer was that if you asked you would get, but if you demanded you would almost certainly be confronted with difficulties. Nominally a DC was in charge of the district of a size often similar to an English county, but his position was largely dependent upon consent. This applies today in many other walks of life, but it is often not realized. It would be wrong to think there was never any friction and there was certainly much good-humoured badinage between different departments on social occasions.

The Agriculture Department was necessarily much concerned with cocoa on which the prosperity of the Gold Coast depended, but there were also problems connected with the local system of shifting agriculture. This consisted of clearing a piece of forest or orchard bush (a term used to describe scrub land with small trees), and cultivating the land cleared by cutting and burning the brushwood. The Forestry Department had the task of trying to conserve the natural forests and maintain conditions for regeneration. The Department did this largely by establishing forest reserves and preventing incursions into them; they did both these things with energy and efficiency.

The Education Department was concerned with the good running of schools. Most of these were run by different denominations of Christian missions, which could be very confusing for village communities, who found rivalries unintelligible; they wanted schools for their children whoever provided them. They were equally keen for the Medical Department to provide dispensaries and visits from government doctors. The doctors tended to be based in hospitals in towns; here the more seriously sick were gathered. Going to hospital was very much a family affair with each patient having a member of the family to cook and look after their general needs.

The Public Works Department tended to be the subject of much innocent merriment, but it is only fair to say that they could teach some useful lessons today on how to manage with slender resources. The use of a road notice reading 'Large Bump' did give some idea of what to expect; it was more useful than 'Temporary Surface'. When wartime shortages led to a lack of roofing felt it was disconcerting for a government officer hoping for his roof to be repaired to come home to find holes being bored in the floor. The idea was to let the water run out. This actually happened and was stated in evidence before a commission set up under a learned judge to enquire into service conditions just after the war. His lordship tended to side with the aggrieved government officer, although holes in the floor were at least a palliative.

As well as familiarising myself with the work of various Government Departments I started on some dull court work concerning debt cases. Criminal cases in the larger towns were heard by a member of the Colonial Legal Service as District Magistrate. In the case of Cape Coast there was one named Scoles. A thing I remember about him was his causing the wrath of Mr Fieldgate, the Provincial Commissioner, by telephoning to say he had ants in his desk. My memories of his

The author outside his first bungalow

wife, Juliet, are happy ones, as she was not only one of very few young ladies amongst the Europeans in Cape Coast at the time, but was also very charming and kind. At the other end of the age scale was Mrs Fieldgate, or so she seemed, although she was only middle-aged. I was a disappointment to her as I did not play bridge and was not available when required to make up her bridge four. This was also a disappointment to Lionel Gardner, who hoped I might have shared this after-hours duty with him.

With the war in Europe going increasingly against Britain and France my work in Cape Coast including trying to learn Fanti seemed increasingly irrelevant. The fall of France in June, 1940, led to a more general realization in the make-believe world of the Gold Coast that things were really serious. The country was surrounded by French territory on three sides and the bulk of the Gold Coast Regiment had embarked for East Africa to fight the Italians, which it did later with distinction. A depot battalion had remained behind, but there were no effective defences against invasion from three directions. There was no particular reason to believe the Vichy-controlled French would invade, but they were in effect under German masters.

My frustrations ended early in July, 1940, when my application to join the Gold Coast Regiment of the Royal West African Frontier Force (RWAFF) resulted in my being commissioned as a 2nd Lieutenant and posted to the newly formed 4th Battalion in Accra. The country was being scoured for ex-servicemen from World War I and some policemen also were being enlisted. There was a fairly good supply of Lee Enfield rifles and an old Vickers machine gun. The latter was assigned the task of defending Senchi Ferry to prevent a crossing of the Volta River.

In September, 1940, the failure of General de Gaulle's forces to rally the French in Dakar to his Free French Forces brought the possibility of conflict in West Africa closer, but his later success in the Cameroons and Chad was encouraging. There was, however, no general inclination on the part of the Vichy controlled West African colonies to join de Gaulle.

The Districts of the Gold Coast and the various Government Departments became denuded of their staff and nearly all organizations gave up some of their staff. The 4th Battalion gathered commissioned and non-commissioned officers from these sources including the United Africa Company (UAC) and Achimota College. Their experience was of a Territorial Army nature, but there was a sense of purpose in trying to do something about a potentially difficult situation. We all shared accommodation in and around the old cantonments mess just outside the town of Accra. This was a wooden building shaken from time to time by aftershocks from an earlier earthquake. Some strange customs and allowances still applied and sharing a room with John Matson, who had arrived on the coast at the same time as I did, brought in the sum of half a crown (12½ p) a night. It was quite a useful allowance in those days as it would purchase about three bottles of the Accra brewed Club Beer. John and I were somewhat surprised to find that it was customary to call for this pleasant beer after the early morning parade before partaking of breakfast. I tested the custom and found it certainly did no harm.

My military duties included being Battalion Messing Officer. This involved going to purchase the daily rations for the troops in Accra. Fortunately, I had a Rhodesian sergeant who had been doing this for some time and he was able to explain where to go and what to buy. The latter seemed to consist largely of Kenki balls, which were basically a corn mixture wrapped in maize leaves. A number of Rhodesians had come to the Gold Coast as officers and NCOs for the Gold Coast Regiment.

A Light Battery

Some tended to have an attitude to Africans approaching that of the South African apartheid, but this sergeant was more mellow than some. Indeed, on one occasion I came upon him unexpectedly in the compound where we made most of our purchases and found him with one of the daughters of the house seated upon his knee. The lady in charge was a typical market mammy with a good grasp of business. She seemed very happy with the entertainment provided by her daughter whilst she gathered together the necessary items.

As far as the writer was concerned spending some four months in the Gold Coast at a time of turmoil was very educative. To my surprise, however, somewhere in somebody's office my previous gunnery training had been noted and in September I received a summons to the Commanding Officer's office to be told I was to go to Zaria in Nigeria where some new batteries were being formed.

CHAPTER III

The Army Brings West African Unity

BEFORE WORLD WAR II there were few formal institutions concerned with coordination between West African colonies. The West African Court of Appeal which heard cases from Nigeria, Gold Coast, Sierra Leone and Gambia was one of the few exceptions. The court was composed of judges from the colonies served and it formed a link between the High Courts of these colonies. It was particularly useful in cases concerned with English Common Law and the Criminal Codes, but the court had to seek expert evidence when Native Customary Law was in issue. The war brought about changes in that a unified military command was set up with headquarters in Accra. At a later stage Lord Swinton was appointed as a Resident Minister to coordinate the West African war effort. It is hardly surprising that his appointment was not particularly welcome to the West African governors who were used to much more autonomy.

I was happy to find myself as part of the increased cooperation in West Africa and sent to Zaria in Northern Nigeria. There was an unexpected hurdle in the need to pass a medical examination. This did not cause me any concern and I fitted in a visit to Dr Gillespie at the European Hospital in Accra whilst rushing around the town to make various personal arrangements before leaving for Nigeria. When I came before the ever cautious and revered Dr Gillespie he declared that my blood pressure was too high. The suggestion that a morning spent dashing around Accra might have some effect was set aside with the words 'Maybe, but you might be getting malaria. Come to see me again tomorrow'. In the event all was well on the next day and I soon found myself being hauled up the side of the Elder Dempster ship *Aboso*. The process was the reverse of being dropped overboard a few months earlier off the *Ada* and it was slightly less alarming than being dropped into a heaving surf boat. Army dress consisting of a bush shirt and shorts with a felt hat was more suitable for the exercise than a suit and Wolsey helmet on the earlier occasion. The beach at Accra was not

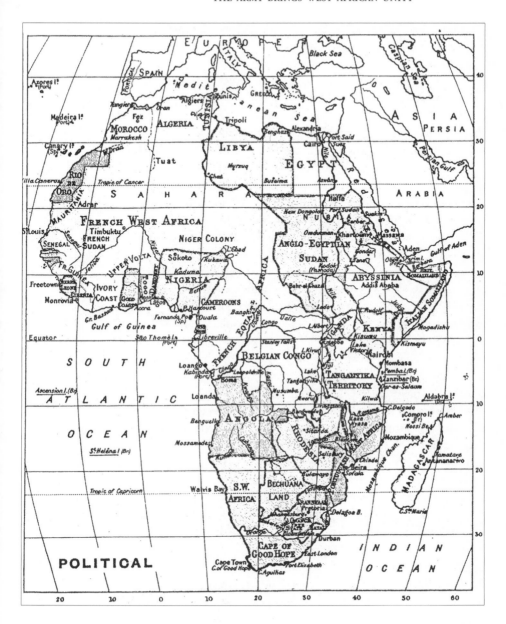

Outline of political map of Africa before World War II

used for much longer, as U Boats began to get into the Gulf of Guinea. Elder Dempster had four passenger ships for the West African service and all were lost during the war.

Also travelling aboard the *Aboso* and bound for Zaria was Major Humphrey Drew. I found him a delightful person. He was one of the gentlemen of the Royal Artillery, some of whom I had met at Larkhill on Salisbury Plain in the University Training Corps. He took charge of gunner training at Zaria for a time, but later went to Sierra Leone and was succeeded by a more brash Lieutenant Colonel who became CRA (Commander Royal Artillery).

Arrival at Apapa wharf in Lagos was a much less dramatic affair than departure from Accra. The general impression was one of a similar country, but there was less of the ebulliance and cheerful shouting that characterized the Ghanaians on the beach. A train for the north was waiting and it arrived in Zaria during the morning of the next day. The first part of the journey was through thick rainforest country. This gradually thinned out into a more savannah type of country generally described at the time as orchard bush. Around Zaria the country had a lush fertile appearance as it has in September at the end of the rainy season which only lasts a few months and reaches its peak in August.

Accommodation for officers and British non-commissioned officers (BNCOs) was in mud houses with grass roofs dotted around the military cantonment. The roofs came down to a low level at the sides and were excellent insulation from the sun. They kept the rain out well too provided that they were frequently replaced during the dry season. Each house was designed for two or more persons, with two bedrooms and a central dining area. Kitchens and servants quarters were in separate outside buildings. There were few furnishings, but we all possessed camp beds and chairs. Some tables were provided.

Initially I was kindly looked after by Captain Crofton, who had been left in charge of the artillery depot when the Nigerian Light Battery went to East Africa. Crofton was somewhat appalled by the problem of forming four new batteries with new recruits from the bush and largely amateur officers like me. He was, however, a good instructor and it was amazing how quickly things came together. I became part of the 2nd Light Battery (later renumbered 6th Light Battery) of which Crofton initially took charge although he was later given a wider training role. He was nicknamed and generally called Pluto. I never knew the reason for this, as he was neither particularly like a king of the underworld, or an outer planet. I believe there was a cartoon dog called Pluto and this may have been the connection, but the name had probably stuck from his training days as army names often did.

Living conditions in Zaria were remarkably good considering the situation in the war in 1940. There was plenty of food available locally including dairy foods from the Agricultural Department farm at Samaru, a few miles outside Zaria. Chickens were the cheapest and most common source of meat. They were not very large, but available in the market at a cost of 5d (2p), or if the cook was very honest 4½d. Social life was not greatly affected by the war and the Zaria Club still flourished with its polo, golf and horse racing. I was able to acquire a polo pony for £6 and for some reason I became eligible for a horse allowance of £5 a month. This was a very welcome addition to my army pay of around £30 a month. The pony's name was Dan Rakumi, which translates from Hausa to 'Son of a camel'. He was quite good with humans, but he did not like other horses. As a result I was not very successful at learning to play polo, since he seemed to think it was good gamesmanship to bite opposing horses on the neck or backside. In the latter case kicks failed to deter him, but they were a bit dangerous for his rider. He could move very fast and I found he could jump quite well, so I entered him for the army race over low fences which was to have formed part of the Zaria Race Meeting, but the CRA had the race cancelled as he thought it was too dangerous; he was probably quite right. Hard riding hats were not in use and it was remarkable how few injuries there were from equestrian activities. My nearest miss was a telephone wire strung between two trees, which I only saw a few yards away when cantering. Somehow I managed to get both the horse's neck and my own underneath it.

Considering the state of the war in 1940 and 41 there was a large amount of social and sporting activity in Zaria, but we did have to work hard. There was much to be done in the way of enlisting and training troops who had been gathered from villages all over Northern Nigeria as well as getting ourselves trained. The 3.7-inch Howitzers did not present any particular problems. The gun drill and firing of them was similar to that for World War I 18-Pounders and the more modern 25-Pounders. The 3.7-inch Howitzers were, however, screw guns designed to be taken apart for transportation. In Northern India this was done by mules and the guns were used in mountainous regions,

Dan Rakumi

but in Africa they were more a general purposes gun and wooden bearers were used so that the various parts of the gun could be head loaded. The larger sections, such as the two sections of the barrel and the recoil mechanism, were carried by four men. The total number required to carry the whole gun was around 30 and there were additional carriers for 26 rounds of ammunition in boxes with 2 rounds in each; altogether over forty men were required for carrying. There were four guns in a battery, so each battery had over 160 men engaged upon carrying only, and another 24 men were required to fire the guns.

When the guns reached their firing positions the various parts were placed in a circle to be taken in turn to be put together. The carriers then departed to the waggon lines; this term was used in the days of horse drawn guns for the area to which horses and limbers were taken. In my days in the Oxford University Officers Training Corps I had taken part in driving teams of horses across Salisbury Plain. It was great fun, but had little to do with modern warfare in its increasingly mechanized state. Teams of gun carriers likewise were hardly a modern concept for 1940, but they were retained for several more years. The batteries from Nigeria and the Gold Coast which went to East Africa for the campaign against the Italians soon adopted the idea of carrying the guns in 3-ton lorries. This was also done when a Light Battery was despatched to the Northern Frontier of Nigeria to support the Nigerian Regiment in the event of a possible French attack that did not occur. This was early in 1941, when British and Free French forces moved into Syria and Lebanon to take over from the Vichy supporting regimes.

The lack of consideration of the problems of using carriers for guns was very frustrating. There were large areas of Africa where horses or mules could not be used owing to trypanosomiasis, the disease carried by the tsetse fly. Head loading was regarded as a way of being able to use the guns away from roads, but it was not possible to use narrow bush paths for teams of gun carriers when the nature of the loads required two men to walk side by side to carry their load on a bearer. Unfortunately, senior officers visiting the gunners seemed interested to see the guns fired without giving much consideration to the logistical problems posed by the African bush. We had a visit in Zaria from General Giffard who was GOC West Africa with headquarters at Achimota in Accra. He gave an interesting talk about his experiences in East Africa during World War I, when the Germans were defeated in Tanganyika, but he did not seem to relate this to the changes that had taken place with road building and motor transport. General Giffard had some ideas about transport in the bush including the use of bush carts on bicycle wheels; the troops found these so difficult to handle in the experimental stages that they preferred in some cases to put the loads and the carts on their heads. Another idea the general expounded was adding salt to water bottles carried on marches to prevent heat exhaustion. This was scientifically based, but there was insufficient regard to the correct amount of salt and the emetic effect of large quantities was overlooked in some cases.

An immediate problem in enlisting and training a large number of recruits from all over Northern Nigeria was one of language. Fortunately, the Hausa language was almost universally understood and the most commonly spoken one; it also had the advantage of being fairly easily learnt by Europeans. We were also fortunate in having amongst the territorial officers one John Coulson who was an education officer in civil life. He took some classes and I found him an excellent teacher for people who were mostly not natural linguists. I remember

he started off with the verb 'kawo' meaning bring. The pro-
nunciation was not exactly the same as 'cow', but if one
pronounced it like that it would be understood. Hausa also has
some very useful words like 'ina' meaning 'where', which could
also mean 'what' in various contexts. Another useful word was
'jirgi' which translates literally to boat, but could be used for
almost any form of conveyance with a suitable suffix. In the
case of an aeroplane it was 'jirgin sama', meaning a boat in the
sky. John Coulson was a colourful character with many friends,
but he was not very popular with his Colonial Service superiors,
as he became divorced twice; in the Colonial Service divorce
was not generally acceptable. Apart from other considerations
it could make postings to different government stations difficult,
if former husbands and wives were not to have to live in the
same town. In the case of John Coulson we had the pleasure
of having him in the Gold Coast after his second divorce which
with typical Colonial Service humour had acquired him the
name of 'Wedding Bells Coulson' in Nigeria.

The troops we had to train were mostly illiterate and had
received very little education in their villages. There was much
more education in the southern parts of Nigeria than there was
in the North. This happened largely through Christian missionary schools and as a result southerners were often employed
in the North on clerical and similar type jobs. This led to some
friction and we avoided using southerners in gun teams, so we
had to train persons who were quite ignorant of sophisticated
instruments on gun sights and other gun mechanism. In theory
every man in the team of six on a gun should be able to carry
out every task, but we were not able to achieve this; we were
lucky if we had a spare gun layer on each gun by the time we
left Zaria in 1941.

Discipline amongst the troops was rarely a problem. They came
from Muslim states with a hierarchical organization and so they
were quite familiar with obeying orders. Northern Nigeria was
the part of Africa in which Lord Lugard found indirect rule

worked. He apparently came to the conclusion in later life that it was a philosophy that could be of universal application in Africa, but it was far from the case. This was noticeable in the southern areas of Nigeria as well as the Gold Coast. British administrators sometimes found it difficult to grasp the problems connected with chieftainship in areas where hierarchical traditions such as those of the Muslim world did not apply.

Training gun carriers was relatively easy and mainly concerned with building of physique to carry heavy loads up to 20 miles a day. The loads were divided so that each man carried a weight approximating to 60lbs. This was generally established throughout West Africa, as the load that a man of normal strength could carry on his head. The carriers were taken with the guns on route marches and on 'drill orders' which were basic exercises in putting the guns into action in different positions from which they could fire. This was less strenuous for the carriers than route marches as they could rest whilst the gunners were putting the guns into action. Despite the heavy nature of their work the carriers always seemed to have energy to spare for song. Their marching songs tended to start with praise for Allah, but they quickly deteriorated into ditties of a bawdy nature. When returning from a march through the 'Sabon Gari' (New Town) near the army cantonment the young ladies of the town came out to see them; they delighted in a song beginning 'Hawa karua ciki ciwon sani'; this translated to 'Hawa, the harlot with gonorrhoea'. There was an even less repeatable song about a man called Dogo Yaya who had suffered an unfortunate affliction to part of his anatomy as a result of his amorous liaisons. When arriving back at the cantonment all blame was laid at the door of the medical officer with a song beginning 'Likita ba shi da kyau' meaning 'the doctor is no good'.

A big problem arose over fitting the troops with boots. They were accustomed to walking barefoot, but this was not really satisfactory for army life and field operations. It may have been a natural feature for African feet to be wider than European ones or it may have been induced by walking barefoot from childhood, but it was a source of a substantial problem. Many of the boots sent to West Africa were too narrow and the Quartermaster Sergeant, a regular British soldier, had a very difficult time trying to fit feet into boots. He found he had to use army numbers rather than names in dealing with his clients, who kept coming to enquire whether their boots had arrived. The Hausa Language was not his strong point and seemed to be confined to 'Numbanka' meaning 'What is your number?'. From anywhere near at hand one could hear this question, followed by a pause whilst he looked at his list, and then barrack room language was used to tell the unfortunate man to go away. His name was Reed, but he became known to the troops as 'Numbanka'; they were generally good at giving nicknames.

We had two other BNCOs (British Non-Commissioned Officers) in the battery. One was a regular Battery Sergeant Major, who was in the general mould of his office, and the other was an Artificer known in gunner language as the Tiffy. He was very good at keeping the guns in order mechanically and he was also good at working with Africans; this was not always an attribute of BNCOs. The ones who had been in India often found it most difficult because they expected everything to work as it did in India. This also applied to regular gunner officers who had been in India. Some came in senior positions and we often found it took them about three months to learn how a battery carried on head loads could not work like a mountain one in India transported by mules. If they did not learn they were liable to become candidates for invaliding out of West Africa; malaria and stomach infections took their toll. The bulk of the officers in Zaria were locally recruited or wartime commissioned officers, some of whom had seen service with the BEF before it was evacuated from the Continent at Dunkirk and elsewhere. There were some experienced Colonial Service Officers from various parts of Nigeria and the difference in experience between those from the North and those from the southern regions was interesting. In the 6th Light battery we had one Neil Mackenzie who amongst other things had been in Aba when there were some quite serious riots a few years earlier mainly led by the women; they were always a force to be reckoned with in the non-Muslim parts of West Africa. I heard a very interesting conversation between Neil and a regular officer with service in India. The major from India said that what he could not stand about West Africa was the way things never worked as they should. Neil replied that was what he found so fascinating and a saving grace rather than the reverse. It was an interesting comment and perhaps one that marked a dividing line between those who could adapt to West Africa fairly easily and those who found it very difficult.

Amongst the colonial service personnel assembled in Zaria there were a number of persons who had been on the same course at Oxford with me before joining the service and others who had undertaken a parallel course at Cambridge. There were other persons with varying lengths of service in the Nigerian Administration. I shared a house (mud built with grass roof) with one Malcolm Milne who had joined the service from Cambridge a year earlier. We had both been members of University Mountaineering Clubs and we did a few scrambles on the bosses of rock which stood out from the plateau around Zaria. These were rendered more interesting by the variety of lizards which inhabited them; we were happy not to encounter any more dangerous reptiles.

The plateau around Zaria stood at about 1000 feet above sea level and the climate was cooler than some of the lower areas around it. The Harmattan Wind blew off the Sahara for four or five months in the winter and made some of the nights much cooler still. The nearest thing to a Hill Station in Nigeria was at Jos, which stood on a plateau about 4000 feet above sea level. A few days local leave early in 1941 enabled me to visit Jos with Malcolm Milne. We stayed at the Hill Club which was much frequented by the tin mining community in the area. They were very hospitable and often invited many folk like us into their homes; these were spacious and well furnished and well kept by plenty of servants. It was all a very pleasant interlude and in Malcolm's case proved to be the beginning of a happy romance with a daughter of one of the mining managers. We travelled in a Morris touring car not particularly suitable for Nigerian roads, but it conveyed us there and back without hitch.

The war news in the first part of 1941 was mostly bad and in West Africa the defence of Freetown, capital of Sierra Leone, assumed some importance. The French were sending

reconnaissance aircraft over the port which was a most important staging post on the sea route round the Cape of Good
Hope to the Middle East as well as India and the Far East.
Some of our gunner officers were sent to man the anti-aircraft
defences of Freetown, although they had not necessarily ever
seen an anti-aircraft gun. I was happy to be left with field guns,
but later the whole of 6th Light Battery to which I belonged
was put under orders to go to Freetown. This was generally
welcomed as a change from the routine of training around
Zaria. I was put in charge of the advance party. I did not have
any particular orders on what to do, but I was despatched to
Lagos with various items of equipment and ammunition.

On the journey to Lagos I was surprised to find myself sought
out and found at one of the stations by Audu Zuru. How he
knew I was on the train I have no idea, but he was a former
member of my section of the battery who had been discharged
from the army with leprosy. He wanted to see me because he
was still owed some money by the army; this was hardly
surprising with the difficulties of adapting the army pay system
to West African conditions. The matter was fairly easy for me
to settle by informing the battery of his location, but I was
much more worried about the leprosy. He had come to me
some months earlier saying that he had a sore place on his hand
which the medical officer had been unable to cure. I went with
him to the medical officer who was helpful, although baffled
by the condition. He arranged for him to go into one of the
few large hospitals some distance away for diagnosis. The next
we heard some time later was that he had been discharged
suffering from leprosy. I was relieved to hear that he was
receiving some sort of treatment, but I found the whole situation
disturbing; unfortunately there was nothing more I could do
about it on my way to Sierra Leone.

On arrival in Lagos I was attached to the coast defence gunners.
The approaches to Lagos were defended by two 6-inch guns
and some lighter weapons at the entrance to the harbour. I was
required to do a period of duty on a rota watching the harbour
entrances from a tower inside the harbour. There were some
worries about submarines as the one available dredger had sunk
after an explosion outside the harbour. It was not known

whether this was caused by a torpedo or a mine, but the latter was thought to be the most probable cause as it became known later that a U Boat had laid some mines at a few points off the coast.

I was glad that nothing untoward occurred during my times on duty as there were no very clear procedures laid down. However, I had a chance of pointing out the need for this after a telephone call from the Harbour Master. He started by saying that at a certain time there had been an unauthorized entry into the harbour. I looked up my notes and found that at that time a Royal Naval destroyer had come into port. It so happened that I had seen it go out an hour or two earlier. In any event one of HM ships would hardly have appreciated a shot across her bows. I never heard the outcome of deliberations on procedures as I had left for Sierra Leone before anything transpired.

My advance party duties ended in Lagos as the whole battery moved to Freetown together. We boarded a ship called *New Northland* at Apapa wharf and reached Freetown in about a week. The First Officer aboard the ship had been torpedoed whilst serving on the *Ada*, which went down in about half an hour with the loss of only about half a dozen lives; such was the efficiency of boat drill in wartime. The *New Northland* in peace time was a cruise ship of about 2000 tons on the Canadian lakes. She was nicknamed the Naughty Nancy as a result of her reputation for the shenanigans of passengers.

CHAPTER IV

Sierra Leone

THE VOYAGE TO FREETOWN was uneventful although very hot. The ship absorbed heat during the daytime and at night it was closed up to maintain a blackout. Arrival in Freetown was at the height of the rainy season. It is a place with plenty of rainfall amounting to an average of over 150 inches per annum; half of this falls in July and August with only a small lessening in September. We were quartered in a hutment camp at Wilberforce several hundred feet above the town; this stands near the water's edge on the large inlet which constitutes the best natural harbour in West Africa. To the south of the harbour there is a peninsula with a mountain range rising several thousand feet in places.

The next three months were spent doing whatever training we could and trying to get our clothes dry in between times. Army gas capes kept out the worst of the dampness, but they were so hot to wear that one became soaked in sweat from the inside instead. The battery was under the temporary command of Thomas Harding, a District Officer from Southern Nigeria. He was a strong and somewhat eccentric character; this was not an uncommon thing in West Africa. Paradoxically eccentricities could be described as essential to maintain sanity. Thomas Harding was also known as Boomer Harding owing to his powerful voice which always sounded above all others. His equipment included non-military items such as plimsoll shoes and an umbrella, and from time to time he came on parade in the early mornings with these accoutrements. On one such morning General Woolner, the GOC of Sierra Leone, decided he would have a look to see how the gunners were shaping. The umbrella was hastily abandoned, but the plimsolls and bare legs instead of puttees were all too obvious. I did not hear that the general in fact said anything, but Thomas Harding soon found himself returned to district duties in Nigeria. He had much to offer the army in enthusiasm but hardly conventionality. He returned to the Eastern Region of Nigeria, where it was fashionable amongst Nigerians to ride bicycles with umbrellas held above them in wet weather – a feat requiring some skill.

The 6th Light Battery was rejoined in Sierra Leone by a colourful character who had left us earlier to strengthen the air defences of Freetown; the port was being reconnoitred by French aircraft particularly when convoys going around the Cape of Good Hope were in port. Gerry Gardner was a man with a refreshing sense of humour and he did not mind telling a story which was hardly complimentary to himself. He explained his return to us as having been caused by his error in opening fire on the first Hurricane aircraft to appear in Sierra Leone. In civil life he worked for a commercial company in West Africa and since the beginning of the war he had little opportunity to become familiar with a Hurricane aircraft. Unfortunately, after his battery had fired the first shot other batteries opened up; happily the fire was most inaccurate, but the pilot was not amused by his welcome. Sadly Gerry Gardner died later in the war after being in action in Burma.

As the month of September progressed the heavy rains of 1941 began to subside and there were days on which it was possible to dry clothes. The troops, mostly used to the much drier climate of Northern Nigeria reacted well to arriving in a strange country. As officers we got to know them better in that they needed our understanding more than in their own country. Their religion was very simple and understandable. Allah was in charge and everything was under his control so it was no use to 'kick against the pricks'.

As far as Europeans were concerned leave to a colder and less enervating climate was still considered necessary by the army after eighteen months in West Africa. This meant for me that I was to be sent in October or November according to the availability of shipping. In the meantime a notice had come around about a scheme for persons serving in the army with flying experience to transfer to the RAF. I had been in the Oxford University Air Squadron, so I applied, but the scheme had been wound up before I reached Britain in October. The ship, the *Oronsay*, arrived in Avonmouth after a voyage in a heavily escorted troop convoy. The streets of the town had smoke candles lining the pavements which were intended to black it out from enemy aircraft. There was a generally dark appearance about everything in Britain, but there was a very helpful attitude to anyone in uniform and a sense of determination and cheerfulness about the country as a whole.

My leave was originally of four weeks duration, but this was happily extended to six weeks. As far as I was concerned the most important event was getting engaged to be married. It was not a whirlwind wartime romance, as Faith and I had known each other from our Oxford days when we both graduated in the School of Geography. After the end of my leave I was attached to an anti-aircraft unit in Ilford. This Essex town to the east of London was shrouded in fog for most of the time. It was very cold in the suburban house in which I was accommodated together with some officers of the battery and a colleague from West Africa. There was no fuel for a fire, but at some earlier stage the bannisters from the staircase had been used for this purpose; the landing too was in a somewhat hazardous condition with all inessential wood removed.

The next phase after two weeks in the fog was at the Gunner Headquarters in Woolwich awaiting shipment back to West Africa. We were supposed to be available at short notice and it was only possible to be absent for a few hours and the Military Police picketed stations for those returning at night. This was very inconvenient for me as Faith had managed to arrange to stay with relatives in London. However, I found that there was a midnight tram back to Woolwich starting on the embankment. My West African bush hat worn in the style of the Australian forces proved a useful disguise and nobody suspected me of belonging to the Royal Artillery. Unfortunately, I was too late to read the orders on the evening before I was due to leave from Marylebone station. I had been appointed baggage officer and I was, therefore, late in collecting the baggage. This would not have mattered, as the army always allowed several hours more than was necessary, but I had the misfortune to meet the Officer Commanding the Depot on leaving. He was furious and ordered me to report to him on return. I did not tell him I was not returning, so I was safely out of his grasp before he could have realized I had not reported, if he ever did.

The journey back to Freetown was made aboard the *Chitral*, a P&O ship in which I had travelled before the war. She was now a Royal Navy Armed Merchant Cruiser armed with 6-inch guns. With some unusual foresight she and other ships of her ilk were built during the inter-war years with gun mountings just below the decks. Later in the war most armed merchant ships of this type were converted to troopships, but at this stage the *Chitral* and similar ships were on their way to the Far East to provide some form of replacement for the *Prince of Wales* and the *Repulse* lost soon after Japan entered the war. The journey to Freetown started just before Christmas and ended early in the New Year. December 1941 had been a grim month with the great destruction wrought on the United States fleet at Pearl Harbour, the invasion of Malaya and the loss of Hong Kong. On the credit side, the Americans were in the war.

The 6th Light Battery was well established in Port Loko, when I returned from leave. Port Loko was about 30 miles north east of Freetown and it stood at the eastern end of the large inlet constituting the harbour; by road the distance was about 60 miles. The town was no longer a port of any significance and the country around it can best be described as orchard bush; it was quite fertile land cultivated on the African system of shifting agriculture with clearances in the bush being used for a few years. There was practically no rainforest in Sierra Leone probably as a result of centuries of human activity, but the rainfall was similar to that in some West African rainforests, although much less than that of Freetown. Sierra Leone fell into two parts in both country and people. There was the rugged mountainous peninsula on which Freetown stood with its more sophisticated people partly descended from freed slaves, and the inland areas with a more tribal society.

The battery was under the command of Major Michael Keatinge, a Territorial Army Officer, who had been in anti-tank gunnery as well as field gunnery. Mike Keatinge adapted himself to West African conditions very well, although he had spent some years in South Africa and considered the system of government there one which worked and in general unobjectionable. He proved very good at welding a diverse group of officers into a team and he was someone from whom I learnt much about administration and management; he was also a politician and for a short time held the Conservative seat of Bury St Edmunds after a bye-election late in the war. Thereafter he retired from politics in favour of farming in Wiltshire. My first task on returning from leave was sorting out the system in the battery office. This had suffered from a loss of a certain amount of paper which was blown out of the windows by a tornado. However, this did not matter too much as there was a headquarters in Freetown turning out more and more orders and exhortations; each set of these seemed to cancel the previous one so the loss of our papers proved no more than a good excuse for not having seen something.

Mike Keatinge was very good at keeping us free to develop our own training without too much interference from Freetown. At the time we were somewhat scornful and amused by his showmanship, but I was certainly impressed by his remarks over a drink one evening that if things looked pretty good 'top brass' visitors and even the lesser ranked staff officers would come, see and go away; thereafter we would be left alone. We had a special guard composed of large men all about six feet in height drilled to turn out for officers senior enough to be entitled to a guard turn out. General Woolner seems to have been particularly impressed. Although a Royal Engineer himself he remarked to his accompanying staff officer 'you can always tell gunner lines, even the stones are whitewashed'.

One thing we could not do was to get any interest in the operational problem of having over a hundred unarmed gun carriers. We realized that if we went to war with any invading force we would have to operate along roads and tracks with our guns loaded into our 3-ton Bedford lorries. A possibility would have been arming the gun carriers for local defence and using them simply for short distance carrying off roads. The problem was well known in Freetown, but it was probably despatched to General Giffard's GHQ in Accra and there found unimportant or too difficult.

We managed to find an area in which we could fire our guns for practice purposes. This was done with the help of Pat O'Dwyer, the District Commissioner, who had useful people called court messengers; in Sierra Leone these persons could be used to warn local people of various happenings as well as to summon people to court. We had to be careful not to leave any unexploded shells in the bush. On Salisbury Plain it was easy to find unexploded shells, but the task in the bush was quite different. Mostly the explosions could be observed, but then there were likely to be unobserved rounds when shots landed in dead ground. For some reason the gunners always called an unobserved round an OU, whereas UO would have seemed more logical. It may have been part of the Army's preference for talking about 'boots black' as opposed to 'black boots'; the logic here was that first you need to know the main subject which is 'boots'.

The Sierra Leoneons in the Port Loko area were more akin to the coastal tribes of the Gold Coast and Southern Nigerians than our mostly Northern Nigerian troops. There was not much fraternization between the Northern Nigerians and the local inhabitants, but a Southern Nigerian driver succeeded in infecting himself with gonorrhoea. He was a very good driver who was driving for Mike Keatinge, but he was relegated to a lorry. I do not think medical science has found a case of infection from a steering wheel, but somehow Mike Keatinge did not like the idea of a gonorrhoeal driver. Generally we had much less trouble from this disease than we had in Zaria where a cynic remarked that our war effort seemed to be largely concerned with family allotments, boots and gonorrhoea. The payment of family allotments back in Nigeria gave rise to some problems, but generally District Officers seemed to be coping with remarkable efficiency considering the problems of tracing the right dependants. Boots were still sometimes a problem, but the troops seemed to be settling into them fairly well and the army quartermasters had learnt that African feet were generally broader than European ones.

An eclipse of the moon illustrated differences between the beliefs of the local people and our mainly Muslim troops. After enjoying a clear evening with a full moon I went to bed and I had slept for an hour or so when I was awakened by an unusually noisy drumming from the town. I noted there was no moon, but then I saw it gradually reappearing from behind the earth's shadow, which causes an eclipse. The drumming continued until a normal full moon was to be seen once again. The next morning a bleary-eyed mess steward boy who came from the town referred to the events of the night with the words 'God make big palaver for we last night; he cover up the moon'. The word palaver is used in pidgin English to cover a number of things. The term in its correct use describes a gathering of chiefs or others for a discussion or conference, but the word became used to describe almost any kind of trouble and it passed even into European use in the expression of 'not my palaver'; somehow this can be more descriptive than 'nothing to do with me' or 'not my business'. It was a very useful word.

The Nigerian troops with their Islamic beliefs were not at all disturbed by the eclipse. They had a general faith that Allah was in charge although from time to time he might do strange things. Two interesting considerations about the drumming are what was its purpose and what beliefs lay behind it. Throughout Africa drumming is well known as a means of passing messages between villages; stories of news going right across Africa by this means are hardly credible considering the great diversity of languages and customs, but it was a well known method of communication. Drumming has also long been associated with state occasions and celebrations accompanied by singing and dancing; drums are also revered instruments in themselves. In the instance of the eclipse of the moon the precise reasons for drumming were probably more obscure, but there was probably a feeling of a need to do something about it. In the background there would have been a religious connection, but European minds were never well attuned to understand the religions and beliefs of Africa, except in the case of Christian and Islamic ones. From experience later in the Gold Coast and staying for nights in villages it would seem fair to say that African relationships with the spiritual world are more easily felt rather than understood. This particularly applies in forest country where villages tend to be surrounded by thick and dark trees and other foliage.

The time spent in Port Loko was for me perhaps the happiest in my brief army career. As a battery we were largely left to get on with our training and we had a commander we could like and respect in Mike Keatinge. However, the strategic considerations or military tidiness required forces to be concentrated in the peninsula around Freetown. We were therefore sent to a newly built camp in the Grafton Valley, presumably named by a huntsman of Victorian days. The country in the immediate vicinity was hilly, but there was more level land further to the north east which was suitable for firing practice in being less populated. The camp was reasonably comfortable and the area as healthy a one as could be expected in Sierra Leone. Singapore had fallen some months before we moved and there was a natural feeling that nothing of the kind must happen to Freetown. General Woolner sent out an order that in the event of a siege there would be no question of surrender. At the time he gave us the news that Polish officers would be joining the West African forces. I had previously never met any Polish people, but two by name Milahowski (probably spelt wrongly) and Dyk joined out battery. They were both very pleasant men to have and tough characters; these two things were undoubtedly good for us. I happened to come upon them one evening talking together when we were out on an exercise. They were naturally speaking in Polish, but they very courteously changed to English, which they spoke fluently, as soon as I arrived. They went on to tell me also very courteously that they had been saying they were not very impressed by British military methods. Poland had of course been engaged in a fight against overwhelming forces and I could quite understand how we could be seen as no match for the Germans. Fortunately, we were only likely to be confronted by Vichy French colonial forces. My Polish friends were kind enough to say they thought we would win the war through what they called the usual British good luck. Once again they were quite right as our army had only been saved from destruction by the English Channel, the RAF and the Royal Navy.

Life in the Grafton Valley was somewhat monotonous for everyone, but in retrospect we can only be considered very fortunate; we had few troubles. We managed to keep the troops busy and we rarely had disciplinary problems. There was a session in Mike Keatinge's office quite frequently dealing with minor disciplinary offences such as being late on parade or having uncleaned boots, but rarely anything serious. I made a point of getting the Sergeants, Sambo Hadeija and Garuba Gorguri in charge of the two guns in my section to deal with minor matters without charges for the orderly room. There was an occasion when Sambo Hadeija had a man who lost his temper and refused to obey an order. There was a certain amount of personal animosity, which I investigated, and dealt with the matter in an unmilitary way without a charge. The man concerned was given what the army called fatigues and there was no further trouble.

There was some civil unrest in Sierra Leone whilst we were in the Grafton Valley; this was mainly related to wages and rising costs for all commodities. We were instructed to be ready to give assistance to the Civil power, if requested. Various manuals were consulted but none gave much help, so we decided there was no substitute for a training exercise. We divided the battery between rioters and law enforcing troops; if we had asked for volunteers there would have been no lack of rioters. It was all great fun which the troops needed and everyone's amusement was increased by the District Commissioner, Christopher Swayne, happening to pass by whilst it was all going on. He naturally enquired what was happening and also enjoyed the situation, although he did not necessarily agree with our methods of quelling a riot. Surprisingly, nobody was hurt beyond a few bruises. Christopher Swayne was very kind to us in asking members of the battery to his house to meet his charming Norwegian wife, who must have found us all rather boring but gave not the slightest sign of this. I went with Neil Mackenzie, a District Officer, from Southern Nigeria, who regaled the party with an account of rioting in Aba, where the women led the rioters.

Neil Mackenzie was a very versatile man. As far as the battery was concerned his great strength was training the drivers to keep their 3-ton Bedford lorries well maintained. We were very proud of our transport and our drivers. There was a small weakness in the ignition system of Bedford lorries in that the condensers attaching the leads to the plugs were liable to jump off the plugs; this put the cylinder concerned out of action. It was fairly simple to hear from the rhythm of the engine when this had happened, but African ears sometimes found this difficult in spite of their natural appreciation of musical rhythm. Patience as always in training was rewarded and Neil had plenty of this. In this aspect of training in Africa as well as in the mechanics of lorries he taught me some very useful lessons.

From time to time various vehicles were allocated to us to see if we could use them for our guns. These included a Bren Gun Carrier, which was somewhat hazardous on the narrow roads, and a vehicle called a Quad. This had a four wheeled drive and had a winch to pull itself out of boggy ground. I was sent out with Sergeant Geddes to try out this vehicle and find a swamp to test it; this was not difficult, but unfortunately we tested the winch to destruction. It broke and left us with the mud literally as well as metaphorically all over our faces. We found nothing better than our faithful 3-ton Bedford lorries. These served us very well with the guns pushed up a ramp into them.

We had a break from the routine of training in the hot Grafton Valley when we went to a firing camp in some open country north east of the Freetown peninsula. Being only about twenty miles from Freetown this gave an opportunity for the brass hats at Headquarters to have a day out looking at the gunners. We did different shoots and I was allocated a close shoot with the brass hats and the General gathered on one side of a ravine and the 'enemy' on the other. Happily Dickie Watson was Gun Position Officer as he knew more about gunnery than the rest of us having been with the BEF at Dunkirk in 1940. It all went well as it had to do. Then I was given a GF Target (fleeting opportunity target to be engaged quickly) in the far distance. Three out of four guns put their shots in the target area, but the fourth caused a rumble amongst the bushes far away on the flank. However, nobody took much notice and the next showpiece was by the coast defence gunners. They were expected to show that unlike the coast defence guns of Singapore they could be fired at targets inland. We all gathered on the side of a hill awaiting the arrival of shots on the other side of a valley. There were some rumbles somewhere in the hills but no signs of anything near the target. I think every gunner present felt sorry for Sammy Allen, the commander of the coast defence battery. Some of us had known him in Northern Nigeria where he was with the field batteries; he was a bank manager in civil life with a great liking for precision. Whether the coast defence guns could have hit the target is doubtful as they were flat trajectory 6-inch guns sited near sea level and not suited for lobbing shells over hills. The Rock of Gibraltar was a site from which coast defence guns could fire inland, but some of these guns were at the top of a precipitous rock. Even then some alarm was caused by Spanish Howitzers placed in a valley near the Straits during the Spanish Civil War.

For most of the time life in the Grafton Valley was one of routine in which the army indulges in either peace or war. There was one bright morning when Mike Keatinge and I were the only officers on parade. The remainder had failed to return from an evening visit to Freetown, which was an occasional event for everyone except the orderly officer; on this occasion I happened to be the one who had to stay behind. It was some time before there was any information about what had happened, but then a message came by the intermittent telephone line to say that the fifteen-hundredweight truck in which they had travelled had been hit by a train. It was very fortunate that the train had only hit the extreme rear end of the truck and simply slewed it round so that it ran into the ditch at the side of the road. Nobody suffered serious injury and the occupants had spent the night as guests of the RAF at Hastings airfield a few miles from Freetown; fortunately nobody knew Gerry Gardner had shot at the first Hurricane to arrive there.

The railway line was a very dangerous one in the way it crossed and recrossed the road running east from Freetown. The crossings were uncontrolled in any way and warning signs could be obscured by encroaching bushes. Trains had a light at the front, but it was quite easy to miss this and it was generally agreed that no blame should be attached to the truck driver or the train driver. The frequent crossing of the road was apparently necessary to avoid steep gradients for the train. In this instance it was a freight train travelling at night but there was a passenger service by day from Freetown to Bo in the middle of the country. Departure from Freetown in the morning was an important social occasion with much shouting and last minute boarding and arrival in Bo was something of a triumph. The Sierra Leone Regiment with pidgin English as its language had a marching song which ran:

> The train for Bo
> No agree for go;
> The engine he done tire;
> He no get plenty fire.

This delightful ditty kept the troops going for many miles and reminded them of home when far away.

An outing to Freetown was not usually as exciting as the one ending in a brush with the train for Bo. The usual evening away from the Grafton Valley revolved around dinner at the City Hotel. This was situated a few hundred yards from the landing wharf in the harbour and was often the first port of call for 'old coasters' returning from leave. It was an old establishment where one felt the atmosphere physically and metaphorically of old Freetown. The hotel features in Graham Greene's *The Heart of the Matter*. The meals were uninteresting, but they were a change from army rations largely composed of tins of bully beef and tins of meat and vegetables; the latter was later admitted in the House of Commons to include a small proportion of horse flesh, but we did not know this at the time. As a town Freetown was an interesting mixture of old shacks and newer buildings; the term 'City' applied to the hotel was somewhat presumptuous. A feature of some prominence was the prison which had a notice reading 'HM Prison – Trespassers will be prosecuted'. West African prisons were hardly very rigorous for the inmates, but it is the only one I saw which had a notice forbidding trespassers. As a magistrate I rarely used the penalty of imprisonment except as an alternative to a fine, but it was sometimes preferred by the accused.

At the end of 1942 the possibility of war in West Africa virtually disappeared as a result of the landings of American and British forces in North Africa. Control of the French colonies by the Vichy government ended and the colonies still under Vichy came onto the allied side in the war. This threw open the question of the future of the West African forces, which now included a division of troops returned from the successful campaign against the Italians in East Africa. It was decided that West African forces would be used in the war against the Japanese in the Far East. There were to be two divisions, the 81st and the 82nd Divisions; the 81st Division was to be formed from troops who had spent their time in West Africa and they were to be the first to go to the Far East. Nigerian troops in Sierra Leone were sent back to Nigeria and early in 1943 we found ourselves in a very large tented camp near Ede (pronounced Ed-day) in open country in Southern Nigeria. The tents were all set up in straight lines and it was very hot inside them. As good gunners we decided to practise camouflage and made ourselves more comfortable by building roofs of palm leaves over the tents.

There was still no decision on how we were to operate against the Japanese with large numbers of carriers striding into the jungle. We were, however, shortly despatched to a forest area between Iwo and Oyo; the idea was to find out whether we could fire our guns in a forest area. Eventually we found somewhere from where we could fire, but there was considerable difficulty over observation.

There was some discontent amongst our troops at this time because they had not been allowed to go on leave. It would have been reasonable to have sent them straight on leave when they returned from Sierra Leone; however there did not seem to be any realization in high places that they had been far from home in alien surroundings. As far as the officers were concerned there was not any detectable enthusiasm for going to the war in the Far East. We had felt ourselves able to deal with anything the French might do against us or indeed to take over French territory if required to do so, but the Japanese were a different matter.

We did not suffer from lack of shade in our forest camp, but there were disadvantages. It was the beginning of the rainy season and tornados in the forest were quite unpleasant. They tended to bring down large branches and even whole trees; fortunately I resited my tent away from a leaning tree that fell later. After the rain the trees dripped for a very long time and the arrival of rain and soft ground encouraged driver ants to become active. A small obstacle like a tent did not deter them from pursuing their intended path. It was often said in the Colonial Service that on moving into a bungalow occupied previously by someone from a different department a forestry officer always started by cutting down or pollarding the trees; from the short period spent living in high forest I could understand this, as the foresters spent a long time in tents in the forest.

There is a tendency to regard a large proportion of West Africa as consisting of high rain forest, but in fact it is a fairly small proportion. The forest in general starts a short distance from the shore and extends varying distances inland not usually exceeding 100 miles. I was happy not to have to spend much time in high forest, as I found the heavy canopy oppressive and depressing. When my spirits were at a low ebb between Iwo and Oyo I was thinking of applying to go on training to fly planes (in practice Austers) to operate as air OPs (Observation Posts). Then one day a colleague, Dickie Watson, who had left the battery to be part of the staff of the CRA (Commander Royal Artillery) in the forest, came and told me I was to return to the Gold Coast Administration. I did not know if I was in disgrace, as I had made myself a nuisance over a number of things such as the troops not being sent on leave and the impracticality of gun carriers in the jungle fighting the Japanese. The CRA was apparently so enamoured of the idea of head loading of guns that he got together a party of officers to load parts of the gun onto their heads. His principle was right in that as a general rule officers should not ask troops to do anything they cannot do themselves, but African necks were accustomed to carrying loads from an early age; one did not see head loading used in Britain for carrying books to school as happened in West Africa.

After various periods of waiting including several weeks in a transit camp in Lagos I arrived back in the Gold Coast, landing this time at Takoradi. I had to travel to Accra and back again in order to be told to go to Tarkwa forty miles north of Takoradi. However, my visit to Accra was quite useful in that I obtained acceptance of Hausa as my local language for examination purposes and I learnt that it had become the policy of the Gold Coast to recall staff from the armed forces. I was not, therefore, being sent back in disgrace. The Gold Coast Government had considered it reasonable to ask for the return of officers on military service to increase production of vegetable oils and other products no longer available from territories occupied by the Japanese.

The experience I gained from three years in the West African forces was most valuable. I was able to obtain some understanding of ordinary Africans living in rural areas and establish some empathy with them. Sometimes in the Administrative Service it could be too easy to hear only the Chiefs and persons of western style education. The main problems of unsophisticated Africans were related to a lack of experience rather than a lack of intelligence. It was easy to think wrongly in terms of the latter, but talking to the troops about the war and what was happening in it brought to light the lack of knowledge of things which we Europeans tended to take for granted. There is perhaps an indication of this in the Hausa language. The word 'jirgi' was used for a boat or canoe which was well known in most parts of Hausa country. This word was later made to serve for a train which became 'jirgin kasa', literally a boat which went on the ground. Later there came aeroplanes which became known as 'jirgin sama', literally a boat up above. The word 'keke' for bicycle is also interesting. It was made to serve for almost any kind of machine, but probably derived from the noise made by the early bicycles seen in Hausa country. A sewing machine was 'keken dinki', literally a sewing bicycle. I remember this well as it was a term I had not heard in my early army days, when I first tried the lower standard Hausa examination. I could not think what sewing and bicycles had to do with each other.

Having learnt Hausa in the army was useful too. Whilst I was never in an area of the Gold Coast where it was generally spoken, practically every town had its 'zongo', in which predominently northern people lived. A walk around there in the evening and a chat to all and sundry was well worthwhile and also enjoyable. One learnt things which might take months to find out elsewhere. These small communities knew what was going on and they loved to talk.

CHAPTER V

The Economic War

THERE WAS PROBABLY too optimistic a view about the conclusion of the war amongst many people in the Gold Coast in the middle of 1943. Government officers were taken out of the forces to ensure the efficient production of commodities no longer available from the Far East, but at the same time thought was being given to the future beyond the end of the war. Sir Alan Burns had succeeded Sir Arnold Hodson as governor at the end of 1941 and he was clearly a forward thinking man wishing to prepare for peace; the appointment of African administrative officers and the setting up of trade unions were examples of this.

On returning to the Gold Coast I had hopes of going to the Northern Territories where I felt my army experience would be relevant in the similarity between the peoples of the Northern Territories and those of Northern Nigeria. I had travelled to Accra from Takoradi by train with a night stop in Kumasi and I was interviewed by Gordon Hadow (later Sir Gordon, Deputy Governor); he told me that my services were needed in Tarkwa in the Western Province. This required a return train journey along the same route to Tarkwa which was only about 40 miles North of Takoradi. Here I was met at the station by Hugh Beeton, the District Commissioner. I had heard from friends in Accra that he had a reputation for efficiency, which filled me with some alarm. I had seen efficiency in the army meaning trying to impress others with superficial things without much substance. As far as Hugh Beeton was concerned nothing could have been further from the truth. I liked him straightaway and he remained a friend until his death some years after his retirement. He was efficient in the true sense of the word and he helped me greatly towards grasping the essentials of District Administration.

The area immediately around Tarkwa had lost its high rain forest, but there was much secondary growth. Further west there was some high rain forest which later became an area for some intensive timber production. Mining was a major activity around Tarkwa amongst the many low hills or ridges in the area. There was a manganese mine of considerable war-time importance, but there were many more gold mines and there was still a gold dredging operation in the district. The mines each had their own accommodation for staff and labour; the latter were regulated by Mining Health Areas legislation, which was generally carefully followed by mines managers. These managers also maintained good discipline in their mining areas and there was little rowdiness or unrest at the time. Many of the labourers came from the Northern Territories and their ambition was to make some money and then return home. There were of course plenty of traders and ladies of the night with every intention of taking their money from them.

Governor Burns was a devout Roman Catholic and he arranged the enactment of prostitution laws on the lines of those in Britain and included in these laws provisions for the deportation of women from outside the Gold Coast if engaged in prostitution. The town of Calabar in the south east of Nigeria was a seaport from which some of the women came, but in Tarkwa the trade seemed to be mostly in local hands. There were only a few prostitution cases that came before me in court and I applied the usual fine of ten shillings (50 pence); recouping this did not entail much work, but any larger fine was liable to be reviewed by a judge. One of my predecessors found himself in an awkward position after the police had rounded up a large number of prostitutes. He remanded them in custody before realizing that he was in charge of the all male prison where they would have to be housed. He thought again and had them brought back to be granted bail. The District Commissioner of Kumasi was confronted by an even more embarrassing situation when he found his office besieged by a large group of prostitutes from Nigeria complaining about their proposed deportation. They said they thought this was most unfair, but if the DC thought their charges were too high they would reduce them in any way he might suggest. He had to send them away unreconciled to their fate.

It is a matter of opinion whether Sir Alan Burns was right in taking the line he did. The women in West Africa were the entrepreneurs of society. They controlled most of the markets in agricultural produce for local consumption and they were the capitalists of this trade; they needed capital to get started and they found a lucrative way of doing this before moving to more legitimate business.

There was also some court business in Tarkwa connected with illicit gin (known by various names such as keliweli). The brewing of palm wine from the sap of palms was quite legitimate and it could be a powerful liquor. It could be made by tapping the palm, but unfortunately the local method was generally to cut down the palm, which was very wasteful at a time when palm nuts were required for export to Britain and elsewhere. Efforts to control this by local bye-laws were generally ineffective, but the Government took a strong line against distillation to make keliweli. However stills were seldom found, so the most usual charges brought concerned only possession of the liquid. The fine for this was normally five shillings (25p) a bottle. I felt sorry for one young man who pleaded guilty and, when asked if he had anything he wished to say, said he had found the bottle lying around somewhere; thereafter he was taking it away to drink it, thinking this was the best thing to do, when a policeman arrested him. It was a law which needed to be enforced as palm wine was quite strong enough and generally wholesome, but its distillate and other distillates were quite dangerous to consumers.

My main duties in Tarkwa were connected with court work, the prison, the issue of gun licences and listening to complaints from members of the public. The issuing of gun licences was one of the few statutory duties placed directly upon District Commissioners; most powers were conferred upon magistrates in which capacity District Commissioners were gazetted to their districts. Being available to any member of the public who wished to see the District Commissioner was most important. Only too often the subjects of complaints concerned family matters or village affairs best handled by the chiefs concerned or by tribunals. However, the complainants often regarded it as most important to have the DC's signature on a piece of paper. Having been to see the DC was a little bit like having been to the doctor and I often wondered whether the queue outside the DC's office or that outside the hospital was the most miserable looking on a Monday morning. In both cases those going away looked happier, so perhaps we achieved something.

Hugh Beeton sent me out on treks to visit the villages in the district and to meet the mining community amongst whom he was clearly well respected and liked. He did not give me any

duties connected with the administration of the states of Wassaw
Fiasi and Wassaw Amenfi, which were the main native authorities in the area; there was also Aowin under the Assistant DC at
Enchi, who was responsible to the DC in Tarkwa. The Wassaw
states were relatively well off financially, but they obviously had
a long way to go before they could stand on their own feet. The
general idea was that the various states should be developed as
units of local government able to deal with the central government. The process of progressing towards independence for the
Gold Coast as a whole was seen as one of building upwards from
local government. A problem was the difference between largely
uneducated, although usually shrewd chiefs, and educated persons
amongst the younger generation who had not much patience
with the chiefs. Hugh Beeton and many district commissioners
like him were trying to bridge the gap between these sections of
society by building on the local government which existed. In
1943 nobody realized how short a time there was to do it.

After I had served under Hugh Beeton for a few months the
time came for him to go on leave at the end of a strenuous
tour of duty. Unlike many he showed few signs of being 'end
of tourish' – a commonly used phrase when leave was imminent.
He was naturally keen to be re-united with his wife and son
who had been in England for the whole of his tour. Wives
often had to divide their time between husbands and children
and in wartime it was very difficult for wives to get passages
back to West Africa after leave. The Beetons had a house in
Croydon which was hit by a V2 rocket towards the end of the
war, but Hugh took this very philosophically by dwelling on
the good fortune that nobody was in the house at the time.
He was that sort of man.

Brian Smith succeeded Hugh Beeton at Tarkwa. He was a very
different person, but an amiable character, who likewise was a
friend of mine until his death in retirement many years later.
He was regarded by some people as pompous and he did at
times give this impression, but he was quite a modest man at

heart. He had more likes and dislikes of people than Hugh Beeton from whom the greatest condemnation I heard of anybody was 'he is a twit'. Brian Smith put on an act at times and like many of us had less self-assurance than Hugh Beeton. As DCs we had a problem in being expected to assume control of almost any situation without having any particular power to do so. We had to exercise some bluff from time to time but depended very largely upon good-will; there was some analogy between an actor and his audience. Brian Smith's wife, Margaret, was less of an actor and blessed with much common sense. She was very kind to me as a young bachelor and unobtrusively gave me some good advice on running a Gold Coast household. We all tended to have more servants than we needed, the minimum being a cook and steward. In the local patois the first was known as 'cuckoo' and the latter simply as 'boy', but it was very bad form when talking to them not to give them their names. The ambition of every steward boy was to have a 'small boy' in the household. I managed to resist this in Tarkwa, but in later days there was a small boy in the house. In Tarkwa I could really have managed with a cook steward as a few people did, but as the Assistant DC I was known in steward boy terms as 'small DC' and small DCs were expected to have at least two servants. It interested me some years after I had left the Gold Coast to hear that my last small boy had become cook and steward for a bishop.

Some of the travelling in the Tarkwa District was made fairly easy by the railway, as there were a number of places within fairly easy reach of stations. The view from a train also gave quite a good idea of the nature of the country and its vegetation. All the original high forest had been removed for agriculture at some time but there was some thick secondary growth. The farming method consisted of clearing a patch, planting crops for a time and then letting it revert to bush. On one occasion I met Frank Harper, the Forestry Officer, beside a recently cleared patch and he aptly described the scene as one of complete and utter devastation. The undergrowth had been cut and fired and the larger trees left to burn. We saw the scene at the stage when some of the stumps were still smouldering. The timber from most trees was not much use except for firewood, but a few useful timber trees were inevitably destroyed. Firewood was not short in the villages, but it was of course saleable in the towns; the economics of such trade depended almost entirely on transport. Some trees were better than others as firewood and some regenerated better than others. The umbrella tree was a remarkable representative of regenerative growth and this species seemed to abound by the railway; the shape of the umbrella tree gave it the inevitable name.

The clearing and firing of bush on a shifting basis was not as bad a method of agriculture as it might have seemed. On the whole fertility was maintained to a reasonable degree and soil erosion in forest country was not a major problem. After land had been cleared there was a certain amount of run off into the rivers and streams, which took away a black alluvial soil. This was dug from time to time and taken to the towns to make vegetable gardens; it became known simply as 'black dirty'. In the bush the soil was dug and mounded with a hoe and the crops were planted on the mounds. There was some maize grown but much of the planting was cassava – a much less nutritious crop. It grew as a root at the base of a tall straight stem; it was some time before I learnt that it was the main constituent of tapioca, known disdainfully at my school as 'frog spawn'.

The Agricultural Department was necessarily largely concerned with cocoa, which was the crop on which much of the economic prosperity of the Gold Coast was based. This crop was threatened in the nineteen forties by swollen shoot disease for which there was no cure. The policy was necessarily one of felling and burning diseased trees, but it was important for outbreaks to be diagnosed as early as possible. As far as subsistence farming was concerned the Agricultural Department only had the resources to run experimental farms and give farmers the chance to visit these. The department had well qualified and highly competent officers, but their resources did not extend to advising farmers in the bush, except on a casual basis. Every farmer anywhere has the same problem in that however expert the advice may be it can only be proved over a long period on the piece of land which he is cultivating. Consequently, it is understandable that little progress was made in improving subsistence farming.

Whilst I was serving in Tarkwa the Italians surrendered to the Allied Forces in Italy. There was a radio rediffusion service in the main towns of the Gold Coast and by some means the radio often became rediffused also on the railway telephone system. Thus I was able to hear about the Italian surrender by picking up the telephone for the six o'clock news. There was much optimism in the Gold Coast at that time about how much longer the war could last and there was a move to get back to a normal eighteen months length of tour. As a result I was sent on leave in October, 1943. I counted myself as being very fortunate in being able to go to Britain to get married in November. Faith and I had not seen each other since the dark days of the end of 1941 and our wedding could hardly have been more different from modern ones. It was indeed an achievement on the part of Faith's family to get together a reception such as we had in wartime. There was none of the modern business of detailed planning for about a year whilst the happy couple are already living together. I had arrived about a week before the wedding and we had a brief talk with the vicar on the evening before the ceremony in Bournemouth, which at the time was full of servicemen including some Americans. Two of these took considerable interest in the arrival of the bride, but declined my father-in-law's suggestion that they should come inside.

We left the reception in a taxi in some style and then found our train at Bournemouth Central Station for Swanage. We started off by getting in the wrong part of the train and this nearly resulted in Faith losing her handbag. However, I recovered this from the left luggage office after being cross-examined on what was in it, including how much money. I had to explain that I had just married the lady so I had not the slightest idea. It was very fortunate we recovered the handbag as it had our ration books in it and we should not have been very well received in the hotel in Swanage without them. It was all quite unlike the modern honeymoon in the Seychelles or some other exotic island, but none the less happy for that. After eighteen months in West Africa and organizing myself for our wedding on my return the November breezes and occasional sunshine of Swanage were most refreshing. After a week there we moved to a rented cottage near my parents in Portesham in Dorset. Later Faith returned to her teaching job in Brockenhurst and I shared her lodgings. Whilst she was working one day I had the interesting experience of getting her weekly egg from the grocers. I had to explain that it was no longer Miss Ede's egg, but Mrs Dennis' egg. This was known as the shell egg in addition to which there was a ration of dried egg of American origin; it was by no means bad for scrambling or cooking, but it was known to its detractors as phoney egg. My leave, like Shakespeare's summer's lease, had 'all too short a date', but it was extended twice owing to delays in the departure of the ship. The position regarding Faith possibly joining me in West Africa later was uncertain as passages for wives were dependent upon sea passages being available and wives had very low priority. In any event the matter was settled for us by Faith becoming pregnant and a pregnant mother was just too much for West Africa at the time. Children were more or less banned in any case. Thus I faced a separated eighteen months or more and Faith had to cope with our very happy event on her own.

Eventually the ship by which the Crown Agents had booked my return to the Gold Coast was ready to set sail. The *Desirade* was a Free French ship and it left like many at this time from the Clyde. We started in a large convoy and inevitably one made comparisons between the crew and general running of this ship and the current practices aboard British ships. The crew were certainly impressive in the way they moved to their light anti-aircraft guns and their boat stations. The officers, however, appeared much more relaxed than those on British ships and they had plenty of time to consort with the passengers – particularly the ladies. Their attentions were not unwelcome to any of us as they were very pleasant people, but one wondered sometimes what was happening on the bridge or in the engine room. At a later stage in the voyage we were a little worried about a somewhat inebriated nursing sister on her first voyage to the Gold Coast who disappeared into the Chief Engineer's cabin. Happily one Dr Johnson from Sierra Leone took charge of the situation with remarkable tact, and the nursing sister was saved from becoming a nursing mother. The same Dr Johnson cured me of sea sickness from this voyage onwards by persuading me to try a glass of sherry when my stomach was uneasy early in the voyage; he explained how a little dulling of the sense of balance helps in such circumstances.

Towards the end of the voyage there seemed to be some doubt amongst the ships officers over when we should reach Takoradi; perhaps the Royal Navy officers in charge of the convoy thought it best to keep Free French captains in ignorance, but the captain of the *Desirade* did not mean to lose the opportunity for a party, so one was held two nights before we reached Takoradi; speeches of thanks to the captain and the crew were duly made. The next day at about noon the escort ships moved at high speed away from the convoy dropping depth charges. It was a spectacular display during which we saw the first officer walking around the deck waving his arms and saying 'We do not know what is happening.'. It was, however, impossible not to observe in non-nautical terms that the rest of the convoy had turned right whilst we had turned left. The escort vessels came back after their foray and things returned to normal; we never knew whether there was a submarine or a large shark. We were probably unkind in our comparisons with the practices in British ships, when the Frenchmen taking us to West Africa had to their great credit continued in the war after the fall of France. We were of course used to British ships aboard which one seldom saw the captain unless he was shouting directions from above to smarten up boat drill. We were mostly separated from our families, but unlike some of the French crew we had not left them in enemy occupied territory. The passengers were mostly in the category of men returning from leave on their own or wives who had obtained a passage after a long wait. One such wife was Jean Russell, who was joining her husband Arthur, a forestry officer. When I met them both some months later and referred to our five weeks at sea Jean quickly corrected me and said 'It was five weeks and six days'. It was a long time to take on a journey which in normal times took thirteen days.

On arrival in Takoradi I was called before Mr E. A. Burner, the Provincial Commissioner, to be told where I was to go. Eric Burner was not a favourite senior officer amongst young assistants, but I never had any problems with him; he was a straightforward man of a large build with a loud voice and he liked things tidy and in accordance with General Orders, which laid down rules for staff. He had a wife, Leah, of a similarly large build, who was quite a kindly person, but she had a somewhat frugal attitude towards entertaining. On one occasion at a dinner party she said she could not understand people complaining about the cost of living as the meal she was serving cost one shilling (5p) a head. Nobody eating the somewhat insipid meal knew where to look or what to say.

After nearly six weeks at sea I did not have any strong feelings about where I was to work. Eric Burner quickly told me I was to go to the west of Wiawso in the north west of the province to set in motion the building of a road designed to open up an area thought to have many funtumia rubber trees. The funtumia tree was a wild tree from which the paraa rubber tree had been bred. The job on the road was to be for about a month to get the work started. Eric Burner slightly diminished the importance of it by saying that if he did not assign me this job he would lose me from the province, as he was slightly over strength in staff for a month or so.

After a bumpy ride westwards from Wiawso I came to the beginning of the road I was to supervise. The line had been surveyed and a little bush clearing done at the beginning. I walked on the line of the road to a rest house at the far end followed by carriers with my loads of camp equipment, clothing, food and drink on their heads; the length of road to be built was about six miles. I had been shown a funtumia tree, but there seemed to be very few on the line of the road, which passed through a cocoa growing area. There was no doubt in my mind that the road could be useful for cocoa, but I wondered about its usefulness for getting rubber supplies for the war effort. However, much development done by members of the colonial service was based on opportunism. A chance had clearly arisen to get a road extension and this had been taken perhaps on rather flimsy evidence. Eric Burner had also taken the opportunity to keep me in his province by giving me the job of starting the road.

The work connected with the road was neither difficult nor particularly arduous but it entailed walking a fairly long distance each day. I found setting a task for each day was the best way to get the work done. There was no incentive so strong as being able to finish work as soon as the stint was completed. It was always the best way of organizing road labourers, but difficult to organize it unless one could do it personally; some headmen were, however, able to work the scheme fairly and effectively. The whole idea was probably contrary to some labour legislation, but there was a tendency amongst District Commissioners to turn Nelson's eye in that direction when it was a question of getting a job done.

Apart from my work connected with the road I found spending about a month in a village rest house a useful experience. I had not spent much time in Gold Coast villages having been in Nigeria and Sierra Leone whilst in the army. In the latter country when passing through villages with troops, who were mostly hard working Northern Nigerians, one could not help noticing the use of hammocks in the shade. By contrast my impression of Gold Coast village life was one of hard-working people. The men were out early in the morning on the farm and there was a daily parade of women with children strapped to their backs fetching water and firewood. There was usually a similar performance in the evening and part of my social life consisted of an exchange of greetings with these ladies. During the day too the women were very active in the villages preparing food. A particularly arduous task was beating fufu, a sticky substance obtained by beating cassava roots in a mortar with large pestles. This was a task often carried out by several women around a large mortar beating in turn. Modesty was cast aside and the job was usually done stripped to the waist with an array of bosoms on view.

There were some men in the villages during the day often working on re-roofing houses during the dry season. A number of older men could often be seen in groups holding discussions; some of these probably came in the category of 'Elders'. Communications with District Commissioners often purported to come from 'The Chief and his Elders', but it was difficult to know how many or what category of persons were involved, as the letters from illiterate chiefs were always written by letter writers; these persons were licensed and supposed to get the chief to touch the pen and make his mark. It was always worth getting to know the letter writers, as they often exercised a considerable amount of influence.

As I was known to be a 'small DC', I had to explain that village matters were not my 'palaver'. I have already explained the usefulness of the term 'palaver'. 'Not my palaver' meant nothing to do with me, 'palaver finished' meant the end of the matter, a 'palaver man' was a man who made trouble and 'make palaver' meant cause trouble.

Life in the villages by no means finished at dusk. The hurricane lamp had generally taken over from candles and there were gatherings around these and quite frequently drumming and singing. A few men were also out hunting at night for which flint lock guns were used, sometimes known as Dane guns. The guns were somewhat dangerous weapons stuffed with gunpowder and any sort of ammunition available such as old

A village scene

nails. Animals killed by these unpleasant weapons were collec-
tively known as 'bush meat'. There was a shortage of protein
in the usual diet so any form of bush meat was highly prized.

There was an erroneous impression amongst Europeans who
did not spend much time outside towns that Africans were lazy.
This idea partly arose from their ability to sleep at any time
when they were not engaged on any particular activity. In the
bush a short sleep in the middle of the day in the shade was
probably very helpful and Africans working on their farms
returned to work later. In the towns it was not as easy to realize
that Africans not working in the midday sun were either taking
a scheduled break or not being supervised; in the latter case
workmen throughout the world tend to behave in a similar
fashion, although in Europe this is normally without indulging
in sleep.

I was quite sorry after a month of living in the bush to get
a message that I was to go to Sekondi as soon as possible to
take up the job of Assistant DC of that district. Life would be
more comfortable, but I was managing quite well without such
amenities as a refrigerator. Water in porcelain pots kept essential
things reasonably cool and most of my food was bought for a
day at a time. Some really cold beer seemed attractive, but even
over that I was managing with bottles encased in wet stockings.

CHAPTER VI

Sekondi-Takoradi

I N SEKONDI I FOUND I was to be assistant to Hugh Wimshurst. He was a DC of long experience, but he was happy to delegate most of the district work to me outside Sekondi and Takoradi, which were soon to be constituted as a single town under one town council. He was chairman of the Sekondi Town Council and regarded the job as the first charge on his time. He was also in charge of the Nzima sub-district based on Axim where there was usually an Assistant DC. Hugh Wimshurst also retained responsibility for Shama, a fishing village which had been put under the DC's direct rule following years of disputes over chieftainship. Wimshurst was a practical man, who had been a ship's engineer at one stage of his career, and he took great interest in setting up a fish curing industry in Shama. He was also proud of his achievement in the Axim sub-district in getting a rice mill working profitably after the Agricultural Department had abandoned it as a hopeless enterprise. I did not have much social contact outside the office with Hugh Wimshurst and his wife, but they were both very pleasant to me and I enjoyed working with him. He was always available for help or advice, but otherwise left me to get on with my work.

There were five states in the district, each under a paramount chief. The main rural area was covered by Ahanta, but there were also Upper Dixcove, Lower Dixcove, British Sekondi and Dutch Sekondi. The last two somewhat anomalously overlapped the town council area, but each had an Omanhene (paramount chief). The states of Upper and Lower Dixcove likewise each had an Omanhene and were historically based upon former British and Dutch jurisdiction in earlier years. There was a land dispute between them about a piece of rocky land which was of little economic value. As administrators we sometimes did not understand the emotional importance of a piece of land. In contemporary Europe Spanish feelings over Gibraltar should perhaps be seen in the same light. British thinking in Africa tended to be more in practical and economic terms; the politics sometimes escaped us, or seemed unimportant.

When outside Sekondi I spent a large amount of my time

in Dixcove. There was an old British fort with a rest house built on top of it, which was well designed to catch the sea breezes. The building was also occupied by bats in the upper areas and by rats in the dungeons; happily the latter seldom came upstairs. I found the bats quite fascinating with their navigation systems, although they had the disadvantage of dropping scatter bombs with an unpleasant odour. Ladies were often fearful of bats catching in their hair, but I never heard of this happening to anyone.

I usually saw the chiefs of Upper and Lower Dixcove separately. Hima Dekyi, the Upper Dixcove chief, used to come to see me on his own in the rest house. He was literate and I enjoyed talking to him. The Lower Dixcove chief was less well educated and he preferred to see me in the village with his councillors present, which was more in accordance with custom. The administrative objective at the time was to get the Dixcoves and the other three states of the district to form a confederacy with one Native Authority for the whole area. The Dixcove chiefs did not envisage any problem over this and they saw the probable advantages of having one large treasury instead of five smaller ones. A disadvantage which was not foreseen by most administrators was that a reluctance to pay a local rate (poll tax) would be much greater if the money appeared to go into a treasury in a town far away. Perhaps this was forgivable in that half a century later in Britain the point came out again when a 'Poll Tax' was introduced.

The plans to build up large Native Authorities was made possible by the Native Authorities Ordinance of 1944, which made provision for Native Authorities to be constituted by Order in Council made by the Governor. Native Authorities could thus carry on functioning even when there was a dispute over chieftainship (a Stool Dispute). The Governor, Sir Alan Burns, had deplored the incidence of Stool Disputes some time before 1944, but it was very difficult to do anything about them. Efforts were made to hedge them around with procedures like serving charges on the chief concerned, but this was not necessarily according to custom. There was a very definite form of democracy in the customary system in that if a large section of the people of any state did not like a chief he had to leave office. This was brought about in various ways, one of which was raising a hue and cry outside the Ahinfie (chief's house), whereupon when things became too uncomfortable he would leave; according to custom he would throw off his sandals and run.

Supervising five small treasuries certainly gave me the impression that one large one would be better. On one occasion in Lower Dixcove I found an entry 'To the missing cash'; the sum was over £10 which was quite a large amount at the time for the treasury concerned. I expressed my disapproval of this form of 'creative accounting'. This term was not generally known at the time and I was glad to find on my next visit that the missing cash had found its way back; I did not ask any further questions.

A weakness of all our administration was the imposition of reforms without a move in the direction concerned coming from the people affected whether at national or local level. Education was turning out an increasing number of people at all levels including the higher ones. For those with higher education it was possible to gain entry to the legal and medical professions amongst others, but there was little scope in either central or local government. After some opposition from the Colonial Office in London Sir Alan Burns was able to appoint two African administrative officers; the move was generally welcomed by the service. One of the persons appointed, Yau Adu, subsequently became a leading civil servant in inter-government agencies after independence. The other was Kofi Busia, a future prime minister removed by a military coup. Unlike Yau Adu he was not particularly successful as an administrative officer, but he was academically brilliant. He received a doctorate from Oxford University and could probably have achieved distinction in the University of Ghana, if he had not been diverted by politics. He had suffered from the lack of opportunity in British times for Africans of his ability to gain political experience. The town councils were the only places where there was any chance for African politicians. The four town councils were represented in the Legislative Council established by Sir Alan Burns, but they were outnumbered by the traditional chiefs. I think it is fair to say the problems were well understood by administrative staff in the districts, but less well appreciated in the Secretariat in Accra and hardly understood at all in the Colonial Office; here high sounding terms like indirect rule prevailed.

In the Administrative Service itself in 1944 there was a large gap between District Commissioners and their Assistants on one hand, and their clerks as immediate subordinates on the other. It was not until the nineteen fifties that executive officers were appointed in between. In the meantime the responsibility given to clerks depended very much on the administrative officers in charge. In Sekondi I had two clerks allocated by the DC to me for most of their time. One of these, Mr Mercer, was capable of something much better than a clerical job, whereas the other, Mr Hammond, was handed over to me as one whose future was in doubt. When addressing clerks we always used the prefix Mr, but much later John Baffoe Hammond became known to me as John. He eventually became a Government Agent (successor title to DC) after independence and incidentally in that capacity secured a job for my former cook as a rest house caretaker. I soon realized that John Hammond had suffered from comparison with his brighter colleague and more importantly from not knowing what was expected of him. He reacted well to a little time and trouble taken over his training and six months later I was able to report that all threats to his career as a clerk should be withdrawn. There was practically no formal training for clerks and training on the job often depended too much on other clerks.

Clerical work generally required a large amount of devilling amongst the files. I was often surprised by what good memories many clerks had in turning up something from many months, or even years, earlier. The usual office system was for letters to be read on arrival by the DC, or Assistant DC, and then passed out to the clerks for filing and return with the relevant references. With this system it often took us a long time to answer what may have seemed quite a simple letter. However, we had to get the answer right. One simple letter with a simple answer I particularly remember concerned a scheme to collect waste paper for shipping back to Britain for recycling. A lack of shipping space made it impracticable, but some months after we had asked everyone to conserve waste paper I received a letter simply saying 'Do you wish the police to go on collecting waste paper in their offices?' I had a vision of the police officers becoming immersed in a sea of waste paper, so I quickly made an appropriate apology for not having told them the scheme had been abandoned. I replied by telephone to avoid wasting more paper.

Towards the end of 1944 there were staff changes in Sekondi. Brian Smith whom I had worked with in Tarkwa took over from Hugh Wimshurst and the Provincial Commissioner, E. A. Burner, was replaced by L. W. Judd. In both cases they brought about an improvement in my social life. I found Wimshurst very pleasant and I enjoyed a good working relationship with him, but I had more social rapport with Brian Smith. Unfortunately his wife Margaret was not with him as she remained in England awaiting the return of their daughter from Canada. Angela had been evacuated there early in the war to stay with an uncle and his family. It was a strain on the whole family, but not an uncommon thing in wartime and the family seemed to have come together again very well by the time Angela had her 21st birthday party in the Gold Coast some years later.

The arrival of Judd and his wife, Dot, who called him Judy, was a great asset from my point of view. Their house was near mine and although I passed it on the way to the beach in the Burner days I was only asked in for an official occasion. Now the ever hospitable Dot was liable to call me from the stoep (a raised verandah) and ask me in for a drink. Dot was not always appreciated by the more formal ladies of her own age, but young folk all loved her. She had been married to someone else before Judy, although she had apparently known him before her first marriage. She had two daughters by her earlier marriage; they had worried her by going off to Czechoslovakia as soon as the war was over. The Judds also enjoyed their golf in the evenings and after meeting at the golf club I was frequently asked with others back to their house. This quite often led to a further invitation to stay for a meal. Gold Coast cooks could always expand a meal and they never minded the cancellation of one, as that meant a little extra for them. The Judds enjoyed having people to their house. Dot liked company and conversation and Judy enjoyed an opportunity to impart his wisdom and there was plenty of it; he was country bred in Essex and had much experience in the Gold Coast in different places. He was good at mellowing criticism over a drink in the evening and for my part he cured me of a civil service tendency to air a problem without suggesting a solution. His words were 'You sent me a letter without a recommendation'. I did not do that again to him or any other senior officer and indeed when in remoter places I learnt the advantages of doing something first and then informing the hierarchy later. One of Judy's great

strengths was his understanding of younger people. I had some
need of this when a Governor's Durbar did not run as smoothly
as it should have done.

A Durbar was arranged to mark the formation of the Ahanta
Confederacy composed of Ahanta, British Sekondi, Dutch
Sekondi, Upper Dixcove and Lower Dixcove. Whilst preparations were being made Brian Smith did all the work on it
himself and left me with all other routines. This seemed a
sensible division of labour, but a few days before the event
Brian Smith was struck down with malaria. He briefed me as
far as possible from his hospital bed and then had to leave it
all to me. Most arrangements seemed to have been made and
I was not unduly worried until the day came. Then whilst
awaiting the arrival of the Chiefs at the sports field I received
a message that there was a dispute between them over the order
in which they should proceed to the ground.

Brian Smith had put his car and his driver at my disposal
so I went to the assembly point for the Chiefs in their palaquins
and regalia. The problem was the Chief of Ahanta thought he
should lead as President of the Confederacy whilst the Chief
of Dutch Sekondi said he should lead because it was in his
town. Quite clearly I should have thought of this a few days
earlier. It was the sort of problem which could be resolved quite
easily after a leisurely morning's discussion. The question now
was how to solve it so that the Governor could be received at
the appointed time. After various rejected suggestions I hit upon
the idea that there should be two columns, one on each side
of the road with traffic going down the middle as best it could.
This was accepted with the Ahantahene leading one column
and the Omanhene of Dutch Sekondi leading the other. Thus
honour and custom were satisfied, but I did not have the time
to get the seating and standing room in the field as well
organized as I had hoped before the Governor arrived. Starting
roughly at the scheduled time, Sir Alan Burns duly congratu-
lated the Chiefs on their good sense in forming the Confederacy.

Sir Alan Burns believed in building up central government
based on sound local institutions. It might have worked, but
there were other outside forces coming into play. At about the
same time as Sir Alan was congratulating the Chiefs, a little

known Kwame Nkrumah was arriving in Britain from the USA, where he had taken a doctorate at Lincoln University and come under American anti-colonial influences. Although the Americans were our wartime allies some of their generals made it plain that they were unwilling to uphold the British Empire; they had not forgotten their own colonial history. As far as race relations were concerned they had of course little in which they could take pride.

An interesting visitor to the District Office was Tachie-Menson, the municipal member of the Legislative Council for Sekondi-Takoradi. He was a well educated man, who took a very measured view of things from an African standpoint. He was in a sense the Colonial Civil Servant's dream for political development. He was prepared to pursue the interests of his people fearlessly, but he was always polite about it; he achieved things through negotiation rather than confrontation. Visitors of a different nature included soldiers who had been sent back from Burma on discharge from the army usually for health reasons. I particularly remember one man who was very indignant when I could not direct him to a job. He seemed to be under the impression as many were later that all he had to do to get a job was to go to see the DC.

There were also visitors who had just arrived from Britain. Some had come with various forms of expertise to advise the Government in Accra, but they were not always aware of African conditions. One subject in which the Government was taking an interest was town planning and I met Maxwell Fry after he had been in the country for a short time. He was very pleased to tell me that the Government had agreed to put a stop on any development until plans had been drawn up. This was fine for an ideal world, but in the Gold Coast there was an urgent need to get something done to improve housing. Maxwell Fry's delight at a 'stop order' gave me an understanding of Judd's remark about a housing scheme I outlined to him. He said 'Let us not have a plan, but get on and do it'.

There seemed to be much American interest in missions in the Gold Coast during the year 1945. Members of various missions passed through Sekondi heading for the Northern Territories. There was The Assembly of God, who had been established for some years and were irreverently known as 'The Asses of God'. Then there were the Seventh Day Adventists known as 'The Seventh Day Adventurers'. A completely new one as far as I was concerned was 'The Coming of Christ Mission'. They were situated in and around Sekondi and applied for a permit to do some singing or dancing in the town. When I enquired from Dale Tristram, the Superintendent of Police, about them on hearing the name he asked 'Coming by what boat'. I had to explain that they were already in town, but we never found out much about them and they did not follow up their application. I wondered later whether some joker had made it all up and sent the letter. Generally speaking missionary work, particularly in education, was wholly admirable, but there were some strange ones engaged in proselytization. At different ends of the scale there were the Roman Catholic Fathers who lived a simple life in the bush and some American-based missionaries who brought all modern conveniences with them.

Whilst working in West Africa I learnt more about sectarianism in Northern Ireland than I have anywhere else. In the army I was regaled with stories of what the British did to my country from a southern Irishman who had, like many, volunteered to join the British Army. In Sekondi there was a Northern Irish Agricultural Officer, 'Spud' Mullen, always known as Spud – I never knew his Christian name. Although generally friendly and hospitable in nature and not particularly religious minded, he was unremitting in his condemnation of Roman Catholics and all their works. Regardless of the company present he would come out with remarks like 'Hell roast the Pope'. Sadly some years later his health broke down and he had to return to Northern Ireland, where he joined the artificial insemination service and was apparently known as the bowler hatted bull. I do not know whether he had problems with catholic cows.

The ending of the war in Europe in May, 1945, brought welcome relief of many kinds, particularly for West Africa in the ending of submarine attacks on shipping. The ending of the Japanese war in August came as a surprise as did the Labour Party's overwhelming victory in the British election in July. The world outlook was changed and in the Gold Coast it became a time of reappraisal. It was clear that things would not just return to a pre-war state, but what the future held was far from clear. Amongst members of the Colonial Service there was a distinct uneasiness. There was not a fear that there might not be jobs, but would they be worthwhile and acceptable to Gold Coast Africans. Then there were the undoubted stresses and strains brought about by wartime family separations. These were of shorter duration than many that occurred during the war, but for members of the Colonial Service they were always part of life.

There was less social mixing with educated Africans in Sekondi than in most other places that I experienced. There was no particular reason for this except that there happened to be few Africans in senior positions in the Civil Service. For my part I did not find the European Club a very cheerful place and I was happy to go from time to time with some of my colleagues to the Optimism Club; this was a very cheerful African club in town as its name suggests. Europeans were always made welcome and delighted the assembled crowd if they were prepared to try to dance the African High Life. It was quite easy really and only required a little sense of rhythm and much stamina. There was a delightful High Life called 'Everybody likes Saturday Night'. It went on and on with the band singing -

Everybody likes Saturday night,
Everybody, everybody likes Saturday night.

It was all good fun and the assembled cheerful African faces showing ebullient enjoyment were bound to dispel all gloom. In some parts of Africa, particularly where there were white settlers, it was thought that Europeans demeaned themselves by taking part in African dances and celebrations. Happily this was not the case in the Gold Coast, where a stand-offish attitude caused resentment more than anything else. Chiefs frequently arranged a dance when a DC or other official was spending the night in a village, and he could be sure to be asked to dance with the Chief's daughter. They always seemed to have plenty of daughters.

The expression 'end of tourish' was well known in the Gold Coast. It was used to describe a general feeling of staleness that set in after about fifteen months. At least that was the somewhat imprecise timing when tours were of eighteen months duration. When tours became reduced to fifteen months the feeling tended to come after a year. Leave was on a generous scale with seven days leave for every month served. This meant in effect with travelling time of two weeks each way by sea that after eighteen months there was an absence of nearly six months from the country. Towards the end of my tour in Sekondi I was certainly aware of the 'end of tourish' feeling. Since getting married on my previous leave Faith and I had enjoyed very little married life which was a strain for both of us. Towards the end of my tour I suffered from my first and only bad attack of fever (as malaria was always known). I spent a week in Takoradi hospital and then returned to work without any recuperative period. Subsequently, I suffered minor recurrences and this rather coloured my outlook on life for the rest of the tour. I had certainly learnt much from the varied work in Sekondi and the District outside, but I wanted to experience work in a bush station which I felt was the real Gold Coast, where ordinary people lived and worked; at that time this was the case for the majority of the Gold Coast's four million people.

The practice of passing the buck was well understood in the Colonial Service. This had unfortunate results for DCs as they were the most usual recipients when there was no other obvious person to do the job; in turn DCs delegated many of the routine jobs to their assistants where the buck stopped. One of these jobs in Sekondi, although I never met it anywhere else, was periodically checking money held in the bank on behalf of the West African Currency Board (there was a common currency in West African pounds in British colonies). The survey was supposed to be carried out by a committee chaired by the DC with representatives of the Accountant General and other nominated persons. It was of course a completely impossible task without many days to spare to do a detailed check. A system had, however, been worked out whereby the bank manager set out what was supposed to be there and a few bundles of notes and bags of coin were counted.

On the last occasion I had to do the job before going on leave to the chagrin of the bank manager it was found that many of the bags of coin in the vault had rotted owing to the damp and heat and there was a large heap of mixed coin on the floor. I had to resort to the expedient of adjourning the meeting for one month; it would have been quite impossible even on our arbitrary system to certify that all the money was there or nothing had 'gone missing' – a term used in the Gold Coast to describe anything lost from a teaspoon to a railway engine. I never heard of the latter being lost, but it must have happened as two were found in the bush when a disused siding was cleared for a new line.

In making the adjournment I planned better than I thought, as by that time I had left Sekondi to go on leave. The timing of leave was still dependent upon shipping and the availability of berths on ships, but unexpectedly I was offered an air passage on the recently started passenger service run by BOAC (British Overseas Airways Corporation – the successor of Imperial Airways and forerunner of British Airways). I went from the Takoradi airfield, which had been much used during the war by the RAF for aircraft sent by sea to Takoradi for assembling and flying across the desert to Khartoum and thus to the Libyan battlefront. The civil airport buildings consisted of a former RAF office and a hangar. The office was used for the reception of passengers and weighing in – a process taken very seriously; everything had to be weighed so it was necessary to put on the overcoat held ready for arrival in Britain. When I had just finished this preliminary weighing an approaching 'line storm' broke. The term 'line storm' was used to describe storms which arrived with heavy black clouds forming a line on the horizon. In Takoradi they generally came in from the sea and in the present case the storm lasted for about three hours and postponed take off until about 11.00 a. m. The later take-off in the Dakota (DC3) aircraft delayed arrival at Freetown and Bathurst where we were to spend the night. We were supposed to arrive at the latter at about dusk, but in fact it was dark and we landed down on an old RAF flare path with kerosene flares alongside the runway. The runway itself was simply laterite – the usual gravelly substance used for roads – covered by a linked chain material.

The next phase of the journey consisted of a bus ride of about twenty miles to a rest house where we were to spend the night. We were hoping for a meal and a short night's sleep before a very early morning call and getting back on a bus to go to the airport, but after the meal we were told we had to await the arrival of the Portuguese consul as he had to endorse our passports for the next night to be spent in Lisbon. Eventually he arrived and we got off to bed. The next day was uneventful with landings at Port Etienne and Casablanca for refuelling on the way to Lisbon. Here we were conveyed by taxis which travelled at great speed to a hotel where we spent a comfortable night. Once again on the next morning we were at the airport at an early hour and this time the take off was punctual. However, once in the air one of the engines started giving a nasty back-firing noise and emitting smoke. Back we went to the airport, where the engine was pronounced serviceable after the fitting of a new sparking plug. All went well with the rest of the journey but it became very cold in the passenger compartment over the Bay of Biscay. The cabin crew were very sympathetic and persuaded the captain to open the flight deck door to let us have some of the hot air from there. The crew were then revealed sitting in their shirt sleeves whilst we had all put on our overcoats. The flight ended at Hurn Airport, a former RAF station near Bournemouth. It had been an occasion on which there was much laughter and very good rapport between the passengers themselves and between passengers and crew who were former RAF men. Apart from the cold over the Bay of Biscay the comfort of the seats and the cabin in general compared quite favourably with some modern jet airliners which have neither leg room nor elbow room.

I was surprised by the beauty of the view of England when landing at Hurn. I had expected early November to be rather bleak, but the autumn colours had not yet faded and contrasted with the past eighteen months in West Africa where the colours apart from the bright blue of the sea seemed to be emerald green or 'laterite' brown. I was met at the airport by my parents-in-law who conveyed me into Bournemouth where they lived. From there I travelled by bus to Bere Regis from whence another bus took me to Dorchester, where my parents met me and took me to a cottage in Askerwell near Bridport. Here I was re-united with Faith in a stone built cottage, which we rented for my leave, and saw my year old sleeping son for the first time. The viewing was by torch and candle light, as the cottage had no electricity; cooking was by paraffin stove and water heating by a boiler which would burn anything and everything. The water came from a spring up the hill by the cottage and we had to boil it for drinking as in the Gold Coast.

We were very happy although without amenities now regarded as essential; there were few gadgets to go wrong. We did not have a telephone in the house, but there was a call box conveniently situated just outside the front gate. There were plenty of services in the nature of deliveries – milk came every day, a baker several times a week, a rabbit was delivered on Mondays and the groceries strictly based on wartime rations came on Fridays. The weekly meat ration consisted of a little over one pound of meat for all of us, but the rabbit made several meals. They were unrationed and the farmers were only too pleased to get rid of them.

The only cloud over our lives was the thought that we should have to separate again at the end of my leave in the spring of 1946. This inevitably raised the question in our minds whether continuing in the Colonial Service was worthwhile. There was no shortage of jobs in Britain in the early postwar years, but I could not really think of anything else I wanted to do. We were living near my parents who were insistent in their advice that I should carry on in my career. Eventually it was decided that we would leave our son, Nigel, with them for part of my next tour of eighteen months, so that Faith could be with me for part of the time. My other decision was to follow my interest in the law and read for the Bar, so I joined the Inner Temple. Making a career at the Bar was not really practicable as one had to live on very little for a long time after qualifying, but I felt it might open doors as indeed it did.

In retrospect it may seem that we were overly worried about the health dangers of taking a young child to the Gold Coast. At the time, however, medical opinion generally was against European children living in the West African climate and there were of course worries over the dangers of malaria and other serious illnesses. There were also possible long term effects of prophylactic medicine which had to be taken in order to keep clear of malaria. As time went on the medical profession became more attuned to children living in the Gold Coast, as indeed they had to do when more and more people took their children. Some years later I remember a doctor pointing out to me that the apparent pallor of children's cheeks in the Gold Coast was nothing to worry about as in Britain much of the rosiness was brought about by the east wind.

Eighteen weeks leave after eighteen months' service was by any account a generous ration, but the end, like Shakespeare's summer's lease, always seemed to have too short a date. Thus it did not seem long before I received a letter from the Crown Agents for the Colonies of 4, Millbank SW1 telling me to sail aboard one of the Elder Dempster ships, the *Tarkwa*; she had been equipped to carry forty passengers as a stop-gap reserve before new passenger ships were built to replace those lost during the war.

On arrival on board the *Tarkwa* I found I was in a cabin for three with Jenkins (generally called Jenks by his friends) of the Posts and Telegraphs with whom I had previously travelled and one Mr Brown described as a Government Dentist. Shortly after Jenks and I had met and agreed that our quarters were much better than we had expected we were asked to meet the Elder Dempster passenger manager in the lounge. He started with bated breath saying he owed us an apology and he then announced that he did not know Mr Brown was 'a man of colour'. He was surprised at our unperturbed reaction. Mr Brown turned out to be a very well mannered young man who had just finished his training as a dentist in Britain, where he had spent much of the war. I mention the incident because it illustrates how a colour bar was much more something in the minds of people living in Britain rather than a reality in West Africa. Academics and others who write about the colonial empire today sometimes tend to assume that we in the Colonial Service were colour conscious people. This was the case amongst white people in general in some parts of Africa, but it was not something applicable to members of the Colonial Service in West Africa.

CHAPTER VII

The Burns Reforms

I HOPE THE HEADING of this chapter will give due credit to Sir Alan Burns as a Governor. In the colonial days Governors wielded great power in their colonies subject only to the British Government in London which appointed them. Governors could greatly affect the course of events dependent upon whether they were minded to keep things moving smoothly with peace and tranquillity in their time, or to be forward looking. Sir Alan Burns was in the latter category, but owing to war conditions he had to spend much time on keeping things running smoothly. However, he was responsible during the war years for progressive measures such as appointing Africans to the Administrative Service and getting trade union officers from Britain appointed to help in the setting up of trade unions. It was unfortunate that the reform of central government only came about in the latter days of Sir Alan's governorship.

The constitution of 1925 with an official majority of one in the Legislative Council had lasted for too long, but reform had to wait until 1946 when a Council with an unofficial majority was established. There were 18 elected members in this council but 13 of these were elected by councils of chiefs; the remaining five municipal members were elected by the towns of Accra, Cape Coast, Sekondi-Takoradi and Kumasi. African nationalists were dissatisfied by the way the constitution still left great power in the hands of the chiefs and it also left the Governor with absolute powers if he should decide to use them; in practice this was likely to be rare. The Governor's Executive Council included six African members, but they were responsible to the Governor rather than the Legislative Council. Briefly, the constitution was quite a big step forward, but much depended on how far the African Council members and the public wanted to make it work.

There had been reforms in local government too in the enactment of the Native Authorities and Native Courts Ordinances in 1944. The idea was to make these bodies more representative and more authoritative, but representation was dependent upon appointment by the Governor rather than by democratic election. Implementation was seen as requiring administrative reorganization. Part of this consisted of bringing the Colony into line with Ashanti and the Northern Territories in having a Chief Commissioner instead of three Provincial Commissioners. The first step was the reduction of the Provinces from three to two, leading later to the abolition of Provinces. At the same time districts were in some cases enlarged and put under a Senior District Commissioner with several District and Assistant District Commissioners under him.

As far as Native Authorities were concerned finance was a very important consideration in their smooth working. In many cases small authorities were running on inadequate means to carry out their functions. The appointment of T. R. O. Mangin (later Sir Thorlief) as the first Chief Commissioner of the Colony brought the question of Native Authority finance to the forefront. Whilst I was still on leave Mangin wrote to me to tell me that on return I would be working in his office on the problem of getting viable treasuries functioning in all Native Authority areas. It was indeed a formidable but interesting task. I started work in the temporary office for the Chief Commissioner in a bungalow in Cape

Loading the
Ford Pickup

Coast in April, 1946; John Hooper was already established there as secretary to the Chief Commissioner and he inducted me into the ways of working. The post of Judicial Adviser had also been established and A. J. Loveridge was in this post. There were three rooms in the bungalow – Mangin was at one end, Loveridge in the middle and Hooper and I at the other end. The office clerks worked in various outbuildings and the arrangements all seemed to work very well as a temporary expedient until a new office was built on a breezy ridge some distance away just outside the town.

My first task was to go around all the districts of the Colony and find out what exactly was happening in the many Native Authority Treasuries. Thereafter it was my job to make recommendations including the way in which standardized estimates should be submitted annually to the Chief Commissioner. I had to equip myself with transport for travelling around the country, which was not easy in 1946. Cars manufactured after 1939 were virtually non-existent in the Gold Coast, so I bought a Ford V8 Pick-up of 1939 vintage. There were Government loans for cars repayable on a monthly basis and fairly generous mileage allowances; these were unfortunately quickly absorbed on the many repairs required by vehicles which had travelled on Gold Coast roads for some years. Many vehicles on the road would undoubtedly have failed the MOT now developed in the UK. I was fortunate in not having any particularly dangerous breakdowns, but burst tyres were a hazard. New tyres were quite difficult to obtain and retreaded ones were not very satisfactory as the treads had often been put on unsafe covers. I had two burst tyres, fortunately at the rear. A more serious breakdown was a front shackle on the transverse spring used by Fords at that time. This very nearly landed me in the ditch, but fortunately I was going slowly over a badly potholed road.

A mitigating factor in breakdowns was the willingness of lorry drivers to help; this extended far beyond one lorry driver helping another to helping anybody in trouble. They were very good at fixing things by unorthodox methods. Even my broken shackle was fixed with wood and wire so that I could limp into Akuse, which was a few miles away. Engine failures were quite common and very often this was caused by the all pervading laterite dust from the road getting into the petrol. The local remedy was blowing into the petrol tank and it was amazing how often this remedy worked. Flat batteries were another frequent occurrence and a push start was always willingly applied by lorry passengers or bystanders.

My night stops were often unscheduled owing to mechanical problems. On one occasion I was visiting treasuries with Alan Cowley on my return journey to Cape Coast. My engine came to an abrupt halt in the rain and none of the usual local mechanical nostrums worked. Fortunately Alan was behind me and with his aid and transport I reached Tantum resthouse where he was spending the night. He had not been in the Gold Coast very long, but after a war spent in motor gunboats and submarines he adapted very quickly and approached everything with great zest; it was impossible to be gloomy when he was around. Alan was one of my friends for the rest of my service in the Gold Coast and thereafter until he sadly died after not very many years. In Salifu, his cook and general factotum, he had the perfect Gold Coast equivalent of Jeeves. After we had spent some time refreshing ourselves with the excellent Club Beer brewed in Accra, listening to the rain on the roof and the waves beating on the nearby beach, Salifu sent Kabba, my steward boy, to announce that our meal was ready. Instead of the usual 'chop ready', he had been briefed to say 'Gentlemen, dinner is served'. I think it was the first and last time I was summoned to a meal by such an expression. The term 'chop' was universally used for food and eating. The word served both as a noun and a verb and there were various theories on its origin. It may have come from the Chinese chopsticks.

In the better weather of the next day my car returned to life and I got myself back to Cape Coast. There was fortunately a garage in Cape Coast run by UTC (Union Trading Company). This was a Swiss company based in Basle, which was probably the best at the time in mending old cars, so I placed my old Ford in their hands when back in Cape Coast. I was much happier in Cape Coast than in Sekondi in that I found more friends of my own age and interests. There were a number of young members of the Administration, such as John Hooper and Alan Cowley and others in different departments, such as Mike Horwood, the Forestry Officer, and Edgar Brooks, a police officer who was tragically killed by a drunken mob a few years later. The small nine hole golf course provided recreation in the evening and

Biriwa Village
with author's 1939
Ford Pickup in
foreground

there were happily a number of people who played golf as badly as I did. I particularly remember Alan Cowley on the golf course as he executed a variety of shots into the bushes and tended to say the one word 'interesting' after each. The caddies were very good at finding lost balls by using their bare toes to pick them out of the bush. Sometimes we had two boys – one carrying the clubs and one out in front spotting, called a 'fronty'.

It was pleasant working for Mangin, first in the temporary office and later in the new offices which were ready in 1947. Johnny Loveridge as Judicial Adviser had been appointed to reorganize the Native Courts, but he also turned his hand and his excellent brain to any subject on which Mangin needed help. He was a member of the bar, whose legal knowledge Mangin found most useful as he himself thought legal things rather tedious. Mangin saw his task as one of getting the old order of local government by chiefs and state councils transformed into some more modern form of local government and getting the Administrative Service organized to do this. My task in the jigsaw was first to find out what was happening in treasuries and make recommendations. I was required to do much travelling, but Mangin was very considerate of my problem in having to do this in an old vehicle on some terrible roads. He was always well aware of the problems of junior staff. He had suffered a tragedy in the death of his wife in England during the war and he had a daughter and a son to consider.

Thorlief Mangin's approach to reforming local government was one of trying to make steady progress in improving existing institutions; in this it was complementary to Sir Alan Burns' reforms at the centre of government. The setting up of a central Colony Administration was intended to have the same coordinating effect as in the case of the Ashanti and Northern Territories Administrations. The policy should have worked, but the years 1946 and 47 were the last of the old ways. There were strong outside influences at work both in the world at large and in local Gold Coast events. The election of a Labour Government in Britain with a colonial liberalism and the rapid moves towards independence for India, Pakistan and Ceylon had strong political influence in the Gold Coast. The world-wide shortages of ordinary things, such as cotton goods, fuel oil, cars and bicycles, led to the situation in which there was money without things on which to spend it. With the aid of Development and Welfare grants there was more money in the government coffers than there had been previously; further pressure on resources came from the money of farmers from high cocoa prices and discharged soldiers with gratuities. The

The Chief Commissioner's Office built in 1947

Ankobra hand
hauled Ferry

cocoa farmers had, however, to contend with swollen shoot disease in their trees and the only way to prevent a devastating spread of the disease was to cut down diseased trees. There was compensation, but this meant that the farmers had money to spend, but no cocoa for perhaps five years and in this respect they were like the ex-servicemen in having lost their way of life. Both groups were discontented as a result and black-marketing in the towns led to much blame being directed at allegedly profiteering ex-patriate companies and at the Government for failure to control all this.

All these sources of discontent became well known to me in the course of my travels. My visits to Accra were infrequent, but I found less appreciation of the general situation in the capital town than elsewhere. There was a requirement for administrative officers to make their presence known at the Secretariat. Sometimes it was only necessary to sign the book at the entrance, but sometimes there was a notice attached to the book requiring reporting to someone. On one occasion I found I was required to report to George Sinclair (later Sir George), which I was quite happy to do. He had spent some years in Ashanti and was generally better informed than many of his colleagues. He later became Deputy Governor in Cyprus during the troubles there and after retirement he became MP for Dorking. When I was about to take my leave George said he ought to let Kenneth Bradley (later Sir Kenneth) know of my presence. The result was an invitation to lunch, which I tried to decline gracefully, but George indicated that I should go. Kenneth Bradley had been appointed as Under Secretary, which was a post immediately under the Colonial Secretary. He had recently come to the Gold Coast from Northern Rhodesia (now Zambia) where he had written one of the early books about the Colonial Service entitled 'Diary of a District Officer'. He later achieved distinction at the Commonwealth Institute of which he was the head for a number of years. On the present occasion I was not very favourably impressed. I somewhat stupidly thought he might want to find out something about what I was doing, but instead I was given an account of how well things were being organized at the centre in Accra. The lack of a good impression on my part was probably reciprocated as my main contribution to the conversation was contradictions. I could not accept the contention that things were going very well with the resettlement of ex-servicemen and I had to counter another of his statements. He said that in his day the best of the recruits to the service were sent to East Africa. My reply was simply one of surprise stating that it certainly did not happen in my day. In retrospect this probably seems like an example of how not to please one's bosses and how not to gain preferment. Strange though it may seem the Colonial Service as a whole, although hierarchical, did not take badly to outspokenness and contrary opinions from its lower orders. There was usually a willingness to listen and to learn.

It is doubtful whether any members of the Colonial Service recognized that 1946 and 1947 were the last years of the old ways of trying to make steady progress. There were problems in getting back to normal ways after the war, but there were great hopes of economic and political progress. In the latter case, however, we had no idea how the political pace would be set for us by African politicians. There had been such persons since the beginning of the century, but they had been of marginal influence.

For me personally 1946 was a landmark in that sea passages for wives to West Africa had become more easily available and Faith was able to join me in October. She travelled in a troopship, the *Empire Ken*, in a cabin designed for two adapted for six. I met her in Takoradi and we were later entertained to lunch by the Judds. Faith was somewhat bemused by Dot Judd with usual good-hearted nature introducing her as Philip's bride. Faith hardly felt bridal as we had been married for three years and she had a son nearly two years old. It was, however, typical of the times in that we had been married for three years, but we had only been together when I had been on leave. It inevitably coloured our views on life in the Colonial Service. Faith had the more difficult side of things in that it was inevitably difficult for her to come to terms with leaving a two-year-old child with her mother-in-law; then she had to adapt to life in the Gold Coast. The process of adaption began on the journey to Cape Coast for which my old Ford behaved perfectly. Faith was interested in the village scenes on the way with sheep, goats and chickens all scurrying across the road and the children all waving. She was surprised by the appearance of the sheep, which looked rather like a cross between an English sheep and a goat. The cemeteries outside each village were also a source of some wondering whether these were the graves of white men in the old days who had gone no further. The cemeteries

Bungalow No. 8 in Cape Coast

were in fact the ordinary village ones planted with crotons, which formed the dreary surroundings. Like yews in British cemeteries they seemed to grow slowly without any attention.

On arrival in Cape Coast in the quite breezy bungalow on one of the residential ridges outside the town there were introductions to Yau, the cook, and Kabba, the steward boy. They were no doubt quite nervous about what Faith would be like; cooks and stewards who could manage 'master' quite well frequently had difficulty when 'madam' arrived. However, they survived until Faith went home about ten months later and for the remaining few months of my tour. Faith wisely adopted a 'softly, softly' approach to everything and there were no real problems. Yau tried to make a good impression on the first day with some cakes containing ground nuts for tea, which was something he had never tried whilst I was on my own. I think the cakes could perhaps best be described as rock cakes, but happily they did not become part of the regular menu.

There was a flurry of social activity after Faith's arrival which she found contrasted with the drabber days of early post-war Britain. However, she found it happily much easier to entertain friends. Cooks and stewards were remarkably good at organizing a meal for several people at short notice. The announcement sometimes quite late in the day that there would be six for dinner caused no more than a request for more market money. Failing all else, there was always a chicken which could find its way into the pot and it was really quite remarkable how reasonably palatable meals were produced from a wood stove with pieces of trees pushed in slowly in a smoke filled kitchen; a delay of an hour or so in calling for the meal whilst appetites were whetted with various drinks did not cause any problems. The Gold Coast cooks and boys functioned best doing things their own way in their own time; attempts by some to make things more efficient or economical almost always ended in disaster. Often in such cases a new and less competent servant had to be found; news that certain masters or madams were difficult spread quickly by the 'bush telegraph'.

Cape Coast was a place with several secondary schools and Faith obtained an invigilating job at St Augustine's, a Roman Catholic School for boys after she had been in Cape Coast for a short time. A little later through Father Fischer who was in charge of the administration for the Catholic Schools in the area she obtained a part-time teaching job at The Holy Child College which was a secondary girls' school. Apart from providing some welcome income the job gave Faith much more insight into African society than would otherwise have occurred. An interesting thing from a teacher's point of view was how much easier it was to teach children from the younger generation of families with some education than those from relatively uneducated families. Perhaps it should be put the other way round by saying that it was much easier for such children to learn. There was also, refreshingly from a teacher's point of view, a great eagerness to learn. In the country as a whole there was an appreciation of the importance of education, but there was not an equal understanding of the time needed for the process to work through to the people of the whole of the Gold Coast. As administrators we thought we had plenty of time, but we were wrong.

When Faith arrived I had not completed my travels visiting treasuries so she was able to see some of the country with me. The old Ford generally behaved well when I was travelling with Faith. The scarp leading up to Mpraeso in the Eastern Province set it a hill start test, as we had to stop when Kabba banged on the front cab from the back asking me to stop. He was in a state of great alarm as his bed roll had fallen out and rolled down the hill; he retrieved it after a search in the bush. At Mpraeso we stayed with Malcolm Milne and his wife (not the Malcolm Milne I had known in Nigeria). They were old Gold Coasters and he suffered from some degree of self-importance; this led him to talk after dinner about his 'contract with the Crown'. I had to explain to Faith later that he was just a DC like the rest of us, although more senior, and in a sense we all had a contract with the Crown in being appointed by one of His Majesty's Secretaries of State.

In Kumasi we stayed with Arthur Spooner, who was a charming host. His wife was in England at the time, but I got to know them both well later. Arthur was something of a father figure amongst young administrative officers of my age. He had a philosophical approach to life in the Gold Coast and laughter was not often far away when he was around. He had a theory that feeling too well was bad for your health in the Gold Coast as it led to doing something silly and getting ill.

This was one of a number of seemingly frivolous theories not lacking wisdom in the background.

From Kumasi we went north to Mampong where we were met by Ambrose Smith, who had joined the Administration after wartime service in the RAF. We had dinner with him, but we spent the night in the rest house. Ambrose was and remained a bachelor. He intrigued Faith with a remark – part of his refreshingly cheerful badinage – about travelling with a wife requiring room for an extra suitcase; Faith thought with some reason she was worth more than an extra suitcase. The rest house required much more than a suitcase. It was a long building furnished only with one long table which was big enough for dinner for at least twelve persons or a board meeting. Fortunately, we were travelling with our own camp bed and all our camp equipment. There was a long verandah with a latrine at one end of this. The equipment of this, as at the time, consisted of a three sided box with a hole in it and a bucket underneath it. On visiting this salubrious spot Faith came back and announced calmly that there was a snake behind the thunder box. Happily we were able to summon a rest house caretaker to evict and execute the unwelcome visitor which was a spitting cobra. Their means of attack on their prey was to spit a liquid into the eyes of the animal which temporarily blinded it. When cornered they had been known to spit at human eyes. They had an addiction to lavatories even when flush pans were installed in later years. The term used in African parlance for such places was 'the small room' and steward boys would sometimes answer the telephone with the information that madam has gone to the small room.

Visiting Ashanti was the last part of my work before submitting my report on how treasuries were running and making recommendations for future improvements. If I had spent more time in Ashanti, I might have observed a much better performance by treasuries in collecting rates. I might also have attributed this to a greater willingness to pay when the rating authority was a relatively small one. My recommendations on the other hand were in favour of the formation of confederacies of groups of smaller authorities. This was, indeed, already the accepted principle of the time, but it led to trouble in refusal to pay because of a feeling that the money went to a distant treasury and would not be spent for the benefit of the area paying the rate. My report was, however, well received by Mangin and also by Sutherland who had recently taken up the post of

Assistant Chief Commissioner. We had now moved into the new offices and the relationships became more remote with the Chief Commissioner at one end of a line of offices and the clerks and telephone girl at the other.

I had more difficulty in establishing a rapport with Donald Sutherland than with any of my other senior colleagues. It was probably largely due to our different natures. He liked absolutely everything on the file in writing and he wrote terse instructions rather than talking over problems. He seldom made a mistake and he was even further from ever admitting one. I regarded his meticulous care as pernicketiness and he did not approve of my neglecting minutiae in pursuit of essentials. We had difficulties when the Native Authority estimates started coming in for approval, as he returned the earliest ones to me with a host of queries on the file. Eventually I got over the problem by putting up two or three files at a time and he gave way under the volume of work. He seemed to worship his files and make sure everything on them reflected his care. He was quite unlike later holders of his office, such as Jack Crawford who used to throw files out on the lawn for the office messenger to collect when he did not wish to see them for a time – it was all good fun for everybody. Sutherland's minutes were also much less refreshing than those of Roy Cooper who once wrote 'Yes, I mean no' in answer to a question framed to expect the answer 'No'. It was quite clear what he did mean.

From Mangin's point of view Sutherland was a most useful assistant as he would make sure nothing that emanated from the office could be faulted and leave Mangin to deal with the broader issues at which he was very good. On one occasion I thought Mangin made an error of judgement. He was invited to a meeting of the United Gold Coast Convention (UGCC) in Saltpond about twenty miles away to the east on the coast. The UGCC later became a political party, but at this stage it was little more than a 'talking shop' for Danquah to express his views on more radical government and getting away from the old chiefly system. Mangin declined to attend. At the time I could not help feeling that nothing would have been lost by just going, wishing them well in their deliberations and taking leave pleading an engagement elsewhere. It would have avoided an arms length approach, but Mangin was a very experienced and competent administrator, and his negative approach was no doubt a well reasoned one.

My work became much less interesting when I had to spend

my time in the Cape Coast Office dealing with Native Authority estimates and other such matters. There was, however, plenty of social life in Cape Coast mostly consisting of dinner parties and drinks parties. It was easy to entertain friends with servants who looked after the arrangements, which they generally seemed to enjoy. One of the larger parties was one held by Judge Jackson as a house warming in the newly built judge's bungalow. He was a widower whose wife had died when he was serving in Nigeria. He had been a District Officer and later transferred to the judiciary. We held much more modest little dinner, or lunch parties. On Christmas Day 1946, we had one of our early meetings with Rodney Bennett, who had recently arrived in the Gold Coast and we have been friends with him and his wife Elizabeth, whom he later married, ever since that time. His wedding in Accra in 1955 was one of the last gatherings of District Commissioners in their white uniforms.

In my spare time I was busily engaged on studying for the Bar. In the spring of 1947 I took some local leave to go to Lagos where at that time it was possible to sit for the remaining sections of Part I. Faith and I travelled to Lagos together in one of the Dakota aircraft on the West African route along the coast between Lagos and Hurn in Dorset. It was a very un-pleasant flight through a tropical storm and for good measure the aircraft leaked down the centre aisle. The flight was at around 8000 feet without pressurization, so leaking was perhaps not a serious matter. In Lagos, as well as passing my examination I met by chance on different occasions Danny (Danford), who was in the army with me, and later my horse Dan Rakumi. Danny had obtained a job with the British Council on leaving the army. Dan Rakumi was being ridden by my former Doki boy and he assured me that both he and the horse were in good health; Dan Rakumi was still liable to bite other horses and was only occasionally used for polo.

On return to Cape Coast I started work for Part II of the Bar examination. I took to starting my studies at 5.00 a.m. as it was cool in the early morning and there was less insect life which made things difficult in the evening; various flying creatures tended to bombard the light needed for reading. Amongst others there were some we used to call sausage flies as they were shaped

like sausages and crawled around the floor after shedding their
wings. On one occasion we had an invasion of moths which
dropped a dust that brought on prickly heat; this Faith found
very unpleasant for a few days. Mosquitoes were in about equal
numbers morning and evening and there were plenty of
malaria-carrying anopheles. At that time we were taking quinine
daily as an anti-malarial drug, but there was news of a wonder
drug called paludrine which was expected to be a prophylactic
if taken once a week. By the time we left the Gold Coast we
found it was effective if taken on the basis of two each day
when in malarial areas.

Creatures which enjoyed the insect life were geckos. They
were small lizards which lived largely on the inside walls of
houses picking off whatever was available. Sometimes they
gorged themselves so much that they fell off. I remember one
occasion when one fell down Faith's neck. I had often wondered
about the meaning of the words 'she screamed' in Victorian
novels. Now I knew, but the novels seemed to suggest that the
phenomenon could be produced by much lesser events. Tsetse
flies were not particularly prevalent in Cape Coast, but there
were a few and we had one under our mosquito net one night
when we went to bed. Faith did not believe me when I said it
would not bite us in the dark, so we had to evict the creature,
which looks and behaves rather like a horse fly. Cape Coast
was also kept free of sand flies by sea breezes and so we did
not suffer attacks by these insects, which resembled Scottish
midges in their biting habits.

Other predators in towns were burglars, usually unemployed
persons from the Northern Territories. The difference between
towns and villages in this respect was most marked. In towns
one had to lock up carefully at night and windows were fitted
with expanded metal to prevent entry through open windows.
In villages it was not even necessary to shut the door. Another
refinement in towns was a need to lock the door of the 'small
room'; otherwise entry could be obtained through the hatch
for the 'Tankas' man to take out the bucket every morning.
The term 'tankas' was a local corruption of town council. The
man himself was not according to custom seen by day except
on Christmas Day. Then the steward boy would solemnly
announce 'tankas man wants to see you', which of course meant
an appropriate Christmas dash had to be found.

On one occasion in Cape Coast one of our neighbours, John
Dickson, was disturbed by a burglar who had gained entry

through the 'small room' hatch. After the burglar had gone with very little loot John telephoned the police. A little later a very noisy lorry arrived with a party of escort policemen in heavy boots. The escort police were a fine body of men, mostly from the Northern Territories, who were excellent as a deterrent to wrong-doers, but hardly men of cat like tread.

I had to go away and leave Faith alone sometimes, as she was working at the Holy Child College, and I employed a Wangara man as a night-watchman on the advice of Kabba, our steward boy. He was a Grunshi and he had a Wangara friend, so I was obliged to take his advice, rather than risk the need for a 'watch night', as they used to be called, being proved by untoward means. He slept on a table on the back verandah, but I found later this was quite unnecessary, as one of the police patrol sent after some burglaries around the residential area also slept on the back verandah.

Faith had to go home to take charge of our son, Nigel, before the end of my tour, but only a few months remained. From my point of view this was a tolerable arrangement, but it was very stressful for Faith to have to leave a very young child and then pick up the strings again. It was also not a practicable arrangement for the future and it worked out badly for us both in that we had to spend the whole of my next tour separated.

We thought it a good idea before Faith left to get some furniture made so that we could gradually accumulate things for a home in England. This brought us in contact with carpenters in the town who had some excellent timber on which to work. They were also able to obtain the services of young apprentices eager to learn the trade and willing to work for years on mundane tasks for little more than 'chop money' (enough to buy food); some of them seemed to spend all their time sawing or planing. The first carpenter we found was named Quansah, but he called himself Pogsway on his shop front; he said he wanted to have an English name. He made the desk on which this book is being written. Later we found a carpenter near the DC's office who called his establishment The Modern Workshop. The main difficulty with Pogsway was getting him to complete his work so that Faith could use part of her baggage allowance to take the desk home. After a number of our frequent calls he complained

A Cape Coast
Carpenters Shop

that we went to see him too often so that 'I have nowhere to lay my head'. He added 'Every day you harry me'.

There were a number of other interesting small trading establishments in the vicinity of Pogsway including one opposite where there was a notice advertising 'house plans and all plans'. There was also a local shoemaker who specialized in using old motor tyres for heeling or soling shoes. This was quite a common practice and a very effective one; the soles usually lasted longer than the rest of the shoes. Pairs of sandals were also made largely out of old motor tyres. Tailors and dressmakers were also available in Cape Coast and on one occasion when Faith was trying to find a dressmaker who had been recommended to her we were given the interesting direction 'she lives in the house next to the latrines'. Both tailors and dressmakers were good at reproducing things from a pattern, and starting from a pair of shorts which fitted the only difficulty arose from putting on weight, but then they were generally made with ample room. There were plenty of mechanics able to fix cars, sometimes in original ways. Often when something was not repairable they resorted to saying 'they make him foolish way'. It is an expression I still use when I find some modern mechanism fails owing to the breaking of a small irreplaceable part. We all learnt something from African wisdom, particularly in using or repairing something which was ready to hand rather than buying some new and expensive gadget. As far as the Gold Coast was concerned it is probably fair to say that it was one of the most advanced countries in sub-Saharan Africa in having a class of small traders and artisans.

There were other interesting characters in the town of Cape Coast. One was a man from the Northern Territories who was used to living with very little water for much of the year. He followed his lifetime ablutory habits of washing himself with his legs dangling in the storm drain at the side of the road and using only a large bottle of water. He usually had a little drop over at the end for a drink. The storm drains were about one foot deep on each side of the road and so care in driving was needed not to drop a wheel into them. Another character was a man who went around with straw in his hair. He was quite harmless but somewhat mentally deranged and I think it was the same man who addressed a European lady with the words 'I want to know you – sexually of course'. He was well known and she was not alarmed, but it made a good dining out story for her. There was a high degree of tolerance for mentally handicapped persons in the Gold Coast and in the courts we took great care not to commit anyone to the asylum in Accra unless they were actually dangerous, and there were very few of these.

After Faith went home to take charge of our son, Nigel, again she set up house for us in a cottage at Appleton in Oxfordshire. Here I was able to continue my legal studies and I was called to the Bar at the end of my leave early in June, 1948. I was able to take an extended leave as during the war any leave not taken was credited for a future occasion. The arrangement of a few months on my own at the beginning and end of each tour was acceptable from my point of view, but it was by no means a solution to family life.

It was unfortunate that a number of my friends, including Alan Cowley, had left Cape Coast before I did. Alan went to Oda, a typical small station in forest country. I spent a week-end with him there and met some of his colleagues. One of these the Forestry Officer, Cansdale, had a great interest in wild animals and he kept a few snakes under his old wooden bungalow. Later he became an authority on certain animals at the London Zoo. The Forestry Department was very good at getting useful work done by the very diverse individuals employed in it. The term 'eccentric' could probably be used for some of them, but eccentricities were an essential part of life in the Gold Coast. A senior officer, D. Stevenson, always known as Steve, who spent some years as Assistant Conservator and then as Chief Conservator played a part in keeping everyone going in the right direction. Steve lived to a good old age in retirement still greatly loved and respected by his former staff, who did excellent conservation work in the broadest sense of the term.

Alan Cowley obviously enjoyed his job in Oda. He had some delightful eccentricities amongst which his dog, 'Socks', must be included. Socks was of mixed parentage as indicated by his three white legs and one black leg. He was of an irrepressible nature and distinguished himself in Cape Coast by taking a piece out of an evening dress being worn by Mary Cooper, the wife of Roy Cooper, Alan's senior officer; she brushed the incident aside most graciously telling Alan that it was an old dress. One of Alan's daily battles with Socks and nature took place when he left his house in the morning trying to light his pipe in a breeze with Socks jumping up at his side. I never quite understood why he did not do the kindling before leaving.

I travelled by sea at the end of October, 1947, to go on leave and enjoyed the refreshing nature of a normal peace-time sea journey. On the voyage I met Tony Townsend from the Northern Territories for the first time. He was interested in my plan to become a barrister and later followed the same path; he was in a sense more successful than me in that he established a practice at the bar whereas I never tried to do this. Being a bachelor until some years after his retirement Tony could afford to spend time earning very little money. After establishing his practice he found working in chambers with both men and women barristers convivial and married Suzanne, one of the ladies in the practice. Tony remained one of my friends until sadly he died some years ago. We never actually worked together in the Gold Coast, but we travelled by sea together on a later occasion and we were frequently in touch in London when he was working at the bar. We both had to make second careers for ourselves after we ran out of time in the Colonial Service. When we met in 1947 it did not occur to either of us that this would happen. In the North there was no inkling of a move against the Colonial Government, but in the Colony there was more of a feeling of unease, although not specifically linked to anything in particular.

CHAPTER VIII

Sir Gerald Creasy's Inheritance

READING ABOUT serious rioting in Accra in the *Sunday Times* at the end of February, 1948, surprised me whilst on leave. I knew there was some unrest around the country, but the severity of events that I have described in the first chapter of this book was surprising; I was glad it had happened in Accra. There had been too much complacency in Accra, where there had been little continuity in Government. Sir Alan Burns had left on retirement in August, 1947, but his successor, Sir Gerald Creasy, did not arrive until the following January; about six weeks later the troubles started.

Sir Alan Burns left with fairly general feelings of goodwill both from the African population and the Colonial Service. He had made it clear that he wanted to see both economic progress and political reform at a sustainable pace. From the point of view of the Colonial Service he was seen as a strong Governor, but at the same time one who thought about matters such as reasonable comfort in housing and other living conditions. Having protested on arrival at the presence of a 'thunder box' in Government House (Christiansbourg Castle) he set about getting improved toilet facilities in all houses as soon as wartime conditions made this possible. Sir Alan's departure was marked by one of the frequent misprints that occurred in the local press. The report describing his leaving read 'two burglars sounded the Hausa farewell'. This was later reported in *Punch* with the comment 'probably glad to see him go'. There were some misprints which made one wonder whether some were a deliberate injection of humour such as one describing the consecration of a marriage with the words 'the marriage was consummated on the altar steps'.

Sir Alan Burns left the Gold Coast in a blaze of glory, but unfortunately his latter days were marred by events following the Kibi murder case as it became known. Nana Sir Ofori Atta had died in 1943 after many years as Paramount Chief of the Akim Abuakwa state, one of the most progressive in the Colony.

He was also a member of the unreformed Legislative Council during Sir Alan's early years as Governor. He was well known to Sir Alan, who sought his advice on many matters. Sir Ofori Atta died in August, 1943, and it was customary six months after the funeral to perform various rites. In ancient times it had been the practice to kill slaves and others so that they could serve the chief in the next world. In this instance the Odikro of Apedwa, Akyea Mensah, disappeared. Various diggings resulted in the finding of a body and although Akyea Mensah was not positively identified eight men were charged and convicted of murder. The trial was before a very well respected judge Fuad Bey of Cypriot nationality, who sat in 1944 with a jury composed of independent persons not connected with the State or its Council. The eight men were sentenced to death which was a mandatory sentence at the time. Appeals through normal procedures failed including a final one to the Privy Council in November 1945. Sir Alan exercising his prerogative in the case of death sentences commuted two of the sentences to life imprisonment shortly after the appeal on the grounds that their association with the murder was slightly more remote than that of the others.

Thereafter Dr J. B. Danquah, who had conducted the defence, began a series of delaying actions. Amongst other applications he made was one for a Writ of Error, which was abolished in English law following an Act of 1873. At the same time he did some political lobbying in Parliament in Britain which led to questions being asked designed to suggest that the trial had not been completely fair. All these things made it necessary for the Governor to delay the executions. Eventually in March, 1947, the executions were carried out in respect of three of the convicted persons, but then had to be stopped owing to an application for Habeas Corpus in the High Court. The application was completely without merit, but the executions had to be halted. One of the convicted persons had died since the trial in 1944 so there were two men only remaining to be executed. Sir Alan Burns commuted their sentences as he did not feel it right that they should be brought to the gallows again.

The whole business was probably more distasteful to Sir Alan and caused him more anguish than anything during his governorship. He was a devout Roman Catholic and he did not like the death penalty, but he had to do his duty and there were no mitigating circumstances in a particularly brutal murder.

With the aid of a dagger through the jaw it was made to appear like a ritual murder, but there have been other theories; one suggests that the Odikro knew too much about certain financial and other affairs of State. The State was situated south east of Ashanti and there was a long history of intrigue in high places. Possibly through past wars with the Ashantis the state had become one of the most powerful in the Colony; elsewhere there were many small and impecunious states without much leadership. Dr Danquah played a considerable part in Akim Abuakwa affairs behind the scenes. He justified his interventions on behalf of the murderers as his duty as their lawyer, but he was also interested in his own political ambitions. He had become leader of the United Gold Coast Convention (UGCC); this movement set out its policies including immediate self government at about the time Sir Alan left. The Kibi murder case gave Danquah an appearance of having some power over the Government, but it was not a popular issue in that public opinion in general was in favour of the murderers meeting their fate. A more powerful person, Kwame Nkrumah, had joined the UGCC as its General Secretary and he later left to form his own party, the Convention People's Party (CPP). He was a strong nationalist with ideas of personal grandeur, a dema-gogue, but not a democrat; he learnt much about communism from G. E. Padmore whilst in Britain, but he was not a committed communist.

This was the inheritance of Sir Gerald Creasy in mid-January, 1948, some six weeks before serious rioting broke out. Popular discontent over shortages of goods and black marketing coupled with discontent amongst ex-servicemen over the lack of jobs and the dismay of cocoa farmers over the cutting down of their trees as the only cure for swollen shoot disease were economic causes of trouble that have already been mentioned. All these things combined to make the task of a new Governor very difficult. A boycott of European stores in February and a hostile press were other factors which led to rising tension.

The events of the 28th February, 1948 were set out in the report of the Watson Commission of Enquiry into the Distur-bances in the Gold Coast. Nearly fifty years later there is a description of events in Accra in Colin Imray's book *Policeman in Africa*. The latter is most valuable in giving an insight into the lack of good intelligence and planning before the actual rioting as well as what happened in Accra. The Watson Com-mission carried out an excellent judicial enquiry as one would expect from a Commission headed by King's Counsel, but the Chairman Atken Watson and the members A. Dalgleish and Dr K. A. H. Murray were not well versed in the African scene. Dalgleish was a trade unionist and Murray was a university don. Their recommendations for political reform gave far too much weight to the views of the UGCC and showed little understanding of the Burns reforms which were described as outmoded at birth.

As far as the police confrontation with the ex-servicemen was concerned the event undoubtedly arose from a lack of regard for the importance of the resettlement of this fine body of men. It was wrongly assumed that on demobilization they would be happy to return to their villages and resettle themselves there. Anyone who had served with them knew that they would be very happy to go back with their gratuities, but get unhappy when these had been spent. There was a need for something more than the rather feeble attempts to help them find jobs when they drifted back to the towns. Something like a resettlement corps, such as that for Polish forces in Britain might have worked, or perhaps training schemes designed to provide the skills in demand. Unfortunately, there was no imaginative thinking.

It is fortunate that before the fateful 28th February Colin Imray was aware that there was a danger of serious trouble. He was able to let the army commanders know this so that help from the military was quickly available to help contain the disorders which broke out in the town. Colin Imray's senior police officers including the Commissioner, R. Ballantine, do not seem to have appreciated the seriousness of the situation, but fortunately there was good support at the crossroads from an Assistant Superintendent, Barry Lane. It is also difficult to understand why there was not a greater degree of involvement of the Administration in the planning for the 28th February. If similar events had been in a district outside Accra the DC would have been at the centre of things and considered all possibilities together with the police officer responsible for the district. A question perhaps unasked and certainly unanswered was whether it was wise to tell frustrated ex-servicemen that they could only present their petition at the Secretariat. They wanted to make their grievances known to the Governor, and having it received by a senior official at the gates of the castle might have been much more satisfying and made it possible for a strong police presence to be concentrated perhaps unobtrusively. It is of course easy to speculate with hindsight, but the important point was the lack of apparent concern by the Administration, which there would have been elsewhere in the country. Later similar troubles in Kumasi were greatly mitigated by the DC, David Allen, taking a central part.

The Watson Commission found to the general satisfaction of other members of the Colonial Service in the Gold Coast that the police action at the crossroads was justified in spite of the sad loss of two lives. A member of the Service had found himself in a very difficult position and he had been vindicated in using only necessary force. Politicians such as Danquah and Nkrumah had made use of the troubles to further their own ends and the Watson Commission seems to have been somewhat misled by them. They thought frustration with the constitution and the lack of representative government were the underlying causes of the trouble; they did not seem to realize that economic problems and the grievances of ex-servicemen were quite sufficient to spark off serious trouble. They spent much time trying to find whether looting in the town started before or after the shooting at the crossroads. One witness who tried to establish that the looting followed the return of people from the crossroads said he saw a crowd and looked at his watch. The Chairman was unimpressed and asked whether he usually looked at his watch when he saw a crowd. It is probable that with the police mostly elsewhere there were plenty of people in the town ready for pickings from stores closed for business, but not very secure, on a Saturday afternoon. There was probably much less organization than the Commission thought.

As a result of the findings of the Commission an all-African Committee was set up under Mr Justice Coussey (later Sir Henley Coussey) to make constitutional recommendations. Setting up the Committee was a positive act by Sir Gerald Creasy as Governor before he left in February, 1949, to take up the post of Governor of Malta. The Watson Commission set the course for the future and lost the last chance to retain reasonable control over pace of political advance. There was a need for slowing the speed at which the UGCC politicians wanted to go in order to give time for educational advance. There was a danger well perceived by the Colonial Service of a small well-educated elite being in charge of the majority of uneducated and unsophisticated persons. It was easy for the Commission hearing evidence mainly from the educated section of society to miss this point and they seemed to do so. At the same time it is only fair to say that they did good work in bringing out the economic and other causes of unrest, although their political interpretation was not so sound.

Before his appointment as Governor of the Gold Coast Sir Gerald Creasy had held senior positions in the Colonial Office; he had also been Chief Secretary to the West African Council and became closely associated with West African affairs. For a period of peaceful progress he could have been a good choice, but he was destined to be a Governor who was governed by events rather than governing. This was his misfortune rather than his fault.

CHAPTER IX

Togoland

NEAR THE END OF MY LEAVE I received the good news that I had passed the Bar examination and I was able to be called to the Bar just before my return to the Gold Coast at the beginning of June, 1948. I found myself posted to Kpandu (pronounced Pandu) in Togoland which was generally regarded as a pleasant posting. I returned by air to Accra from the recently established Heathrow airport. At that time it was largely composed of Nissen huts set up as lounges and reception buildings. The somewhat Spartan conditions were offset by a warmth of welcome from the BOAC (British Overseas Airways Corporation) staff, who made one feel that looking after passengers was important to them. The aircraft was called a York for some reason, but it was in fact a converted Lancaster bomber. It took a fairly direct route to Accra with stops at Rome, Tripoli, Kano and Lagos. Tripoli airport still perpetuated Benito Mussolini's name in being called Castel Benito. It consisted of a number of hangars with a room set aside for passengers; everyone had to leave the aircraft whilst it was being refuelled with the high octane petrol used for the Merlin engines. Whilst in the hangar I met Reginald Saloway (later Sir Reginald) for the first time. He was a former Indian Civil Service Officer who had been appointed as Development Secretary. Sometime before the riots in February he had promised his wife that he would not take a job anywhere with racial conflict. The riots made it seem that the promise had been broken, but in fact it was soon apparent to me on returning from leave that there had been remarkably little damage to race relations amongst the population in general.

Arrival in Accra was about 20 hours after leaving Heathrow. I collected my old Ford Pickup and shortly after driving away from the garage in Accra I found everyone rushing into the street with much shouting. My first thought was of another riot, but then I saw most of the people were women and children; they seemed unlikely rioters. In fact the rush was caused by one of the many aftershocks of the Accra earthquake which occurred nearly ten years earlier.

I spent the night in Accra with Richard Walker, who had

been DC in Cape Coast when I was there. He now had the job of Cocoa Rehabilitation Commissioner, which was the designation of the person in charge of the cutting down of disused trees; it was of course a highly contentious political subject used by Nkrumah and others to breed discontent. Richard Walker was an excellent man for the job as he combined unflappability with a friendly attitude towards everyone with whom he worked. He was unlikely to be upset by a group of irate farmers, or by members of his staff finding their job stressful. At the same time he would send everyone away with a feeling that he had listened to them.

My plans for travel to Kpandu were disrupted by heavy rain. I had intended to have lunch at Akuse with Bill Caldow and then go on to Kpandu where Tom Hindle was waiting to hand over to me. Kpandu was part of the enlarged Ho, Kpandu, Keta District which Tom was taking over as Acting Senior District Commissioner, so he was anxious to hand over the Kpandu part of the district. The area was oblong shaped, about 20 miles wide from east to west and about 40 miles long from north to south. It was bounded by the Volta River in the West and by the line of hills marking the French frontier in the east. In getting to Kpandu by road from Accra it was necessary to cross the ferry on the Volta at Senchi. Heavy rain was liable to put this out of action and on this occasion it enforced a night's

Senchi Ferry across
the Volta River

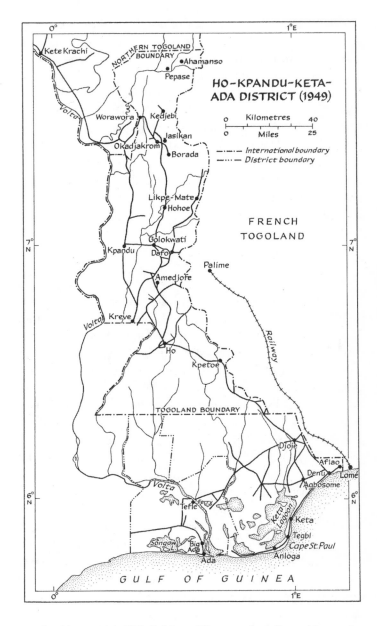

HO–KPANDU–KETA–
ADA DISTRICT (1949)

stay in Akuse with Bill Caldow. He was, therefore, able to give me a full account of the riots in Akuse during which my friend Jimmy Chalmers had been injured. Jimmy had subsequently gone on leave and handed over to Bill, who had been preparing to take over at the time of the riots.

I had a hurried hand-over from Tom Hindle on the next day as he had to leave for Ho. There were, however, some handing-over notes in accordance with the custom during the frequent changes of staff which were part of our life in the Gold Coast. My dreams of administering a small district with my main attentions directed towards Native Authorities and Native Courts were quickly shattered a day or two later. Nobody had told me that Dr David Scott was arriving in Kpandu with a team of smallpox vaccinators. He arrived in the town expecting to be able to start work immediately, but found that nobody seemed to expect him. Happily Tom Hindle had made some arrangements, but as usual there was a need to see they worked on the actual day. This was all soon remedied, but it was part of the pattern of outside events continuously being the source of much of my work in the district.

Togoland could be said to have all the problems general to the Gold Coast and a few more. Some additional problems arose from the fact that Togoland was now under United Nations Trusteeship. This led some politically minded people to form an organization called The Togo Union; the main object was the unification of French and British Togoland. For some years there had been an All Ewe Movement designed towards the unification of all the Ewe (pronounced Ev–vay) people. These included the people of the Keta District which formed part of the Gold Coast before the division of German Togoland between Britain and France after World War I. The Ewes were not a cohesive people like the Ashantis, having moved from the east into their present lands in small groups, and the All Ewe Movement was not particularly active. The people of the Keta District had lived with a frontier for a long time and they had learnt to make the best of it. Many found it a profitable phenomenon for fairly petty smuggling and currency deals; nominally there was exchange control on both sides of the border, but nobody took much notice of it and the market rate prevailed. Control of movement by people across the frontier was only superficial at the policed crossing points and non-existent on the many bush paths. Controls were not the source of any real hardship to anyone; in this they were quite unlike the controls exercised in recent times by Spain on their neighbouring European Union members in Gibraltar. However, at the time there were persons outside West Africa who regarded the Ewes as people cruelly divided by colonial regimes. In retrospect the division of both the former German colonies

Native Court
Registrars outside
Kpandu Court
House

of Togoland and the Cameroons can only be regarded as somewhat high handed after World War I.

Before I arrived Tom Hindle had accepted an invitation to address an inaugural meeting of the Togo Union in Kpandu. We went to this meeting together, but we tactfully withdrew after Tom had made some congratulatory remarks praising their interest in Togoland affairs. Having attended this meeting was very useful for the future as Togo Union members came to see me from time to time to tell me what was going on at least in so far as they felt able to do so. Amongst other things they interested themselves in a European lady by the name of Lalage Bown who was on the staff of the University College in Accra (later the University of Ghana). She was concerned with extra-mural studies and was regarded by some, particularly in the police, as subversive. For my part I found her activities all rather amusing; she was alleged to have said at one meeting that the Romans were good colonists unlike the British as they left some decent roads behind. I think she found travel to Togoland, where DCs were responsible for the roads, rather hard going. On another occasion there was a policeman at one of her meetings. She started by saying how nice it was to have a policeman taking notes; he spoilt it all by saying 'I am here on duty'.

When the Native Authorities Ordinance of 1944 was passed the future of Territories such as Togoland under League of Nations Mandate was not clear, so the Ordinance was not applied to Togoland; there may also have been other reasons for this. In 1948 the Chief Commissioner, T. R. O. Mangin, decided it was time to bring Togoland under the Ordinance and also to apply the Native Courts Ordinance. He decided to make a visit to talk to the existing authorities himself in the hope that they would be happy to come under the newer Ordinances. As a preliminary to Mangin's visit I had talked to the authorities in my district about the matter, but when he came there was an unexpected reluctance to accept the Ordinances as they stood. Mangin wanted to integrate Togoland as part of the Colony, but the influence of the Togo Union had been brought to bear in the district. They did not want anything which would detract from whatever advantages they might obtain from being under UN Trusteeship. Eventually a compromise which I had suggested was accepted; the new Ordinances to be passed in exactly the same terms but with the insertion between the words Native Authorities and Ordinance of (Togoland under United Nations Trusteeship).

At the time of Mangin's visit I was living in the rest house, as the old German bungalow was being modernized. I intended to sleep in the round house – a spare rest house with a grass roof – so that Mangin could have the relative comfort of the rest house. However, he insisted on sleeping in the round house, although I warned him that it leaked. He always showed great consideration for his staff and after a night of heavy rain and a leaking roof he cheerfully said he was experienced at getting his bed placed to avoid leaks. The old German bungalow was built of stone at the beginning of the century and the Germans clearly regarded their station at Kpandu as well placed for defence. There were steep slopes down to the Volta River to the west and eastwards the bungalow provided a good observation point as far as the Togoland mountains; these were formerly German but now constituted the boundary between British and French Togoland. When modernized the bungalow had a new lounge and mosquito proofing for the bedroom; it was a very pleasant house with perhaps the only disadvantage being the need to climb 28 steps from the road below.

As an aftermath to the riots of February and March I had a court case awaiting me in Hohoe (pronounced as nearly as I can describe Hof-way). There were fourteen accused charged with obtaining goods by false pretences. When they heard about rioting elsewhere they went around the main stores in Hohoe asking for supplies of beer and kerosene to give to persons coming with intent to loot. In some ways it was quite an interesting case, but hearing it was somewhat tedious. Every Tuesday morning after dealing with minor offences and most often pleas of guilty, I had to await the wheeling into court of crates of beer and tins of kerosene before proceeding with the main case brought by the police. The court house was a large grass-roofed open-sided building and the local interest in the case led to breeze being excluded by crowds around the edge. After hearing thirteen prosecution witnesses against the fourteen accused over a period of several weeks I was happy to find a way of dismissing the case. One of the fourteen accused had used a kerosene-fuelled lamp to lighten the path of one of the very few policemen left in the town back to his station. It seemed to me that this evidence from the policeman rebutted the contention that the goods had been obtained for unlawful purposes. The expected looters never arrived, so the good faith of the accused was never tested. In my own mind I had little doubt that the accused thought that they ought to get anything going rather than let persons from Accra or elsewhere have it. At the same time nothing but ill-will would have come from a conviction; in any event the case was not beyond reasonable doubt.

There was a more exciting scene in the Hohoe courthouse a few weeks later. There was the noise of a crash in the roof a few feet in front of the bench and some pieces of wood and a cloud of dust came down. The court was adjourned in an undignified manner by the words 'get out'. There was a rapid response to this through the open sides. I continued proceedings from the verandah of the rest house nearby, but for some weeks until repairs had been effected cases were transferred to Kpandu. This was not a very satisfactory solution as most cases arose in Hohoe which was the commercial centre some fifteen miles away.

Hohoe would really have been a more suitable centre for the district headquarters, but nobody suggested it; Kpandu was a much pleasanter and cooler place to live and it was quite easy to spend a few days each month in the Hohoe rest house. The chief in Hohoe, Gabusu, was not particularly high in the hierarchy of chiefs, but he presided over the only town likely to be at the centre of any trouble in turbulent times. I enjoyed good relations with him when I had accustomed myself to his puckish ways and his moderate addiction to the pursuits of Bacchus. On a visit to his courthouse early in my days in the district I tripped slightly on an old piece of chain on the floor in the doorway. The looks on the faces of the councillors present varied between amusement and feigned horror. I was quickly told that I had disturbed a fetish and they would have to perform a customary ceremony to appease the fetish. Briefly, this meant that I had to provide a bottle of gin and I was told it would be satisfactory if I sent it over after the meeting.

On a later occasion when visiting Hohoe I went to see Ian Hastwell who was the John Holt's agent. He was in earnest conversation with another European, who shall be nameless, and I was greeted with the words 'Just the man we want to see'. This was ominous as they were usually quite cheerful people, so I wondered what was the tale of woe. There had been a Gold Coast Legion dance in Hohoe during the previous week at which I had seen them both. Now there was an accusation that Ian's friend had assisted a young lady into his pick-up vehicle and some improprietary behaviour had taken place; he had in fact invited her to have a cigarette in the fresh air during an interval. On hearing the story I have to confess that I burst out laughing. This surprised them, but I explained that whilst I knew sexual inter-course in an open place was an offence according to native customary law I was getting to know Gabusu quite well too. I explained that the whole affair would have to be settled with a bottle of gin, preferably Gordon's. John Holts supplied a bottle of Gordon's to the alleged delinquent and he and I went to see Gabusu and his elders. We duly explained that nothing unto-ward had really happened, but we had brought the bottle so that they could pour a libation according to custom if they thought fit. A minute drop of gin was poured on the floor, some customary words were spoken and we withdrew. Thereafter no doubt a good time was had by all and we were able to refresh ourselves elsewhere with a cold bottle of beer.

The customary law relating to sexual intercourse in an open place was essentially Akan law which became written into legislation regarding cases triable by native courts. The old Akan custom was for a person coming upon two persons 'in flagrante delicto' to put crossed sticks by the path. Future passers by added sticks so that eventually there was a little heap. One can imagine the reaction in the village to the question 'who was it?'. There was probably no need for criminal proceedings. As far as the Ewes were concerned I am uncertain whether it was ever part of their custom, although it was written into the law; we British administrators sometimes fell into error through not knowing enough about Ewe customs. They were kindly people and their young ladies were often very attractive. Features and names showed that this had not been missed by earlier generations of Europeans who had come to the Gold Coast. One prominent citizen was descended from a former Chief Commissioner and was very proud of it. There were also many sharing Danish, Dutch and Portuguese ancestry.

I was never lonely in Kpandu. I had so many visitors that I was glad of the occasional week-end with nothing much happening. One very welcome visitor was Jan Wardzala who was the engineer responsible for the road which was to be built in the north of the district to Pepase to enable cocoa to be exported without the need for head loading by carrier. As things stood at the time it was a walk of twenty miles to Pepase, a journey which took me about seven hours with a number of rests on the way. The Chief of Pepase was of course delighted by the prospect of a road, but his senior chief who lived just north of the same river and about five miles to the east was upset. He tried to prove to me that he had just as much cocoa. Jan Wardzala solved the problem for me by finding a short crossing of the river half way between the two villages which would save money on the bridge and leave enough for the road to branch north of river to both villages. Jan was a former member of the Polish forces in Britain married to a charming Scottish wife, Rita.

On one occasion when I was expecting Jan's arrival a car drew up bearing Alec Dickson, who had been appointed to start a mass literacy campaign, being tried out in Togoland; the idea sounded impressive and was no doubt good window dressing for the UN Trusteeship Council. Alec Dickson had been due to arrive during the following week, but he said he found he had time to come earlier. I was living in the rest house at the time and the only other accommodation was the small round house which had now been re-roofed. I had arranged for Jan to sleep in this and have his meals with me. When I told Alec this he cheerfully said 'I do not mind sharing the rest house with Jan'. There was of course the consideration that Jan might not have felt the same way, so I solved the problem by asking Jan when he came to share the rest house with me and sending Alec off to the round house. He came to dinner with me and Jan and kept up with his steady stream of conversation throughout the evening. He had done some quite interesting things including being a correspondent in Berlin for the Daily Telegraph. After dinner he carried on with hardly a pause and I regret to record that when Jan was taking the strain I put my hand over my eyes and briefly succumbed to sleep. I pulled myself together quite quickly hoping he had not noticed and then got into conversation about his next visit. Whilst I was doing this Jan fell into a cat nap; then Alec said sadly to me 'now he has gone to sleep'. Alec was a great enthusiast and later took a leading part in Voluntary Service Overseas. I met him briefly once after I had left the Gold Coast and now I can only admire his success in motivating young people.

The problem with the mass education programme and also with the whole community development initiative was its maintenance. The getting together of groups of people for a few days as part of a mass literacy campaign was not difficult, but maintaining a programme in the village was impossible without supervision. Similarly schemes to provide materials such as cement to villages with the intention that they should build schools and do other useful work was doomed to failure without supervision. It was often blandly assumed that DCs would oversee self-help schemes, but there was not the time for the detailed work required over a wide area. There was a film produced in Nigeria entitled 'Daylight at Udi', which showed a successful self-help scheme run by a District Officer named Chadwick; this apparently worked well, but it was clear that he was present at daylight. In Gold Coast districts many DCs, including myself, had experience of visiting places and enquiring what had been done with the cement provided. The well known answer was 'We have made cement blocks'. It was often very difficult or impossible to locate these blocks and sadly DCs somewhat cynically called self-help schemes help yourself schemes.

There was not much time spent by DCs, unlike many managers today, sitting around in committees discussing what we ought to be doing. There were certain obvious priorities, one of which was the maintenance of law and order and general public tranquillity in the district. This was usually not very difficult, but it required anticipation of where trouble might arise and being at any possible trouble spot in good time. The responsibility was of course shared with the police who most often saw the first signs of trouble and settled it. On one occasion I returned to Kpandu to be told that all the police had gone off to a riot in an area where I had no idea that any trouble was brewing, but all was well, it was only a fight after a football match. In a different category was a land dispute around Worawora in the north of the district. This conflict was on the border between the Kpandu District and the Krachi District in the Northern Territories. Michael Gass was the DC there and we showed our faces in the area from time to time and held a pleasant social meeting in Kpandu discussing this and other questions. Michael was one of the few Administrative Officers who managed to continue in the Colonial Service after independence in Ghana, and was later Sir Michael Gass, Governor of the Solomon Islands, in the latter days of colonial rule.

I am sure I was by no means alone amongst DCs in taking a somewhat cynical view of mass education and self-help schemes. Both were excellent ideas, but the resources required to make them work were not available. My personal feeling was that more effort needed to go towards local government, the administration of justice by native courts, the development of the agricultural economy and education in schools and for adults in agriculture. A move in the agricultural direction had been made shortly before my arrival in Kpandu in setting up pig keeping at the prison. My previous knowledge of pigs was extremely small so I was heavily reliant, as for all agricultural matters, on Deryck Westwood; he covered the whole of southern Togoland with the help of a few agricultural survey officers to help with the campaign against swollen shoot disease in cocoa.

In the prison in Kpandu we had about ten weaners but after a short time it was clear that one was failing. Deryck told me that we ought to slaughter that one and this was duly done.

The Keeper of the Prison sent a monthly report to his Director with a copy to me and duly reported the slaughter of one pig. This surprisingly to me brought a telegram from the Director asking for a report. I was somewhat irritated as it seemed to me that he was trying to run pig keeping in Kpandu from Accra. Later a pig became sick so I sent him a telegram asking for advice. There were a few more exchanges on a file headed Pigs in Kpandu Prison. Some years later one of my successors in Kpandu, David Heaton, told me how this file had given him much amusement. According to his account there were a number of telegrams reading along the lines 'Cannot advise without veterinary opinion', 'No vet available but pig worse', 'Regret pig dead please advise on post-mortem', 'You should arrange for this if possible'. The telegrams ended abruptly. I met the Director some months later in Accra about a different matter and we had a good laugh about the pigs.

A revered predecessor of mine at Kpandu was Captain Lilley who was DC there for seventeen years between the World Wars. He had lost one arm in the war, but by all accounts he was a powerful character much loved by local people. Most of the substantial bridges on the roads seemed to have been built under his supervision apart from a few which dated back to German times. Captain Lilley also seemed to have had some disagreement with the Director of Prisons. In a letter to his Provincial Commissioner he wrote that he had heard that a wall was to be built around the prison, but he could not imagine a greater waste of money. No prisoner had ever escaped, or tried to do so, or as far as he knew wished to do so. By the time I was in Kpandu a wall had been built and one prisoner did escape. He disappeared from a gang out at work whilst the warder was looking the other way or perhaps sleeping under a tree. I do not think the prisoner was ever seen again, so he probably went across the border to French territory. The escape enabled the Keeper (KOP) to make his unforgettable report 'All correct, Sir – one prisoner escaped'. Although magistrates dutifully sentenced malefactors to imprisonment with hard labour using the letters IHL in the record book, the labour was not particularly hard. Imprisonment was most usually an alternative to a fine and in some cases this was a preferred option with full board and lodging. Thus we had a system translated from Europe which probably did little towards reformation or the prevention of further crime. However, it might have done less harm than some systems in Europe which enable young offenders to learn from experienced old hands.

There were some other files relating to the days of Captain Lilley. One was somewhat incongruously entitled 'Jolly Dance and Burning Bush'. The only possible connection that I could see was that there were people wanting to stop both. In the case of burning bush the Forestry Department was against the customary burning during the dry season owing to the damage it did to sapling trees. At a later stage a more practical approach was found to be getting the burning done early in the dry season so that there was a less hot and damaging fire. Captain Lilley seemed to think stopping either activity was impossible and in the case of the jolly dance he was not convinced that any harm came from it. The dance could perhaps be described as a 'coming out' for youngsters of both sexes, but its nature seems to have been somewhat removed from that of a coming out ball for debutantes in Britain; the behaviour of both sexes seems to have been somewhat less inhibited when the ball was over. The term 'jolly' was quite interesting as a young man referring to his girl-friend could sometimes say 'she is my jolly'.

Whenever I asked the question 'who built that' in the Kpandu District the answer was sometimes 'the Germans', but more often 'Captain Lilley'. He had some very substantial bridges to his name, although they were built at a time when vehicles were less heavy and there were less of them. In my time I achieved one bridge with the aid of a contractor, but I was better at small culverts for bush roads; these were reliant upon the trunks of trees as cross pieces and open ended petrol drums for water to run through. Putting a culvert often led to a bush path being turned into a dry season road. Such roads were known as Chief's roads and were maintained by the chief beating gong-gong and calling out the young men to clear a way for vehicles through the bush. The system worked well in contrast to self-help schemes relying on supplying materials which often 'went missing'.

I might appear to do a certain amount of ancestor worship in respect of Captain Lilley whom I never met, but I also felt some degree of envy in that he had the time in his years in the district to do a proper job; he was able to know and administer his district as opposed to being an agent of central government for schemes thought out – often inadequately – in the Secretariat or 'scratch box' as we used to call it. Significantly, before self-government the term 'Government Agent' was substituted for 'District Commissioner'.

I should like to have had more time for agricultural matters, but many of the resources of the Agricultural Development had to be devoted to cocoa. In Togoland Deryck Westwood was the only qualified Agricultural Officer, but there were Agricultural Survey Officers to help control swollen shoot disease in cocoa trees. Happily there was not much swollen shoot in Togoland, but there was an outbreak a few miles south of Kpandu and Deryck Westwood sought my help in persuading the farmers to have diseased trees felled. I went to the village and found quite a hostile assembly of farmers only one of whom actually had any diseased trees. They started by telling me that on no account would they agree to any trees being cut. Eventually I managed to make it clear to them that only a few trees on one farm had to be felled and that compensation would be paid to the farmer; I said this was necessary to prevent the disease spreading to all their farms. Quite suddenly the mood changed and they were all telling the unfortunate farmer that he must agree to his trees being cut down. I felt very sorry for him as I left, since I could see how this sort of situation resembled foot and mouth disease in cattle in Britain. As a native of the cow rearing county of Dorset I knew how devastating this was, whatever compensation was paid. Trees and cows are not the same, but there was no difference in principle.

Apart from their activities connected with cocoa the Agricultural Department tried to improve rural practices by demonstrating what was possible in Agricultural Stations. One of these was situated in Kpeve about twenty miles south of Kpandu. I visited Kpeve quite frequently and I was always most hospitably received by Deryck and Margot Westwood. They also demonstrated to me that it was quite possible to raise a child successfully in a bush station, as their infant daughter obviously

Kpandu
Health Centre

flourished in spite of forebodings shared by many including myself about having children in the bush.

I was not often able to return the hospitality of Deryck and Margot, but there was one occasion on which they came to lunch and stayed for the week-end. It all started when their pick-up truck developed a horrible grinding noise underneath and it was unable to get up the hill to my house in Kpandu. They stayed for the week-end in the rest house and eventually I took them home to Kpeve on Monday afternoon. Deryck returned some days later to collect the vehicle which could not be repaired until a spare part was obtained from Accra. There was very little one could do to entertain one's friends except supply food and liquid refreshment. Fortunately, I had good stocks of the latter and there were always supplies of chicken and various vegetables in the market. On one occasion I sent Kabba, my steward boy, across to the rest house with a bottle of cold beer, but he returned with the message 'Madam say, bottle stop'. I am not quite sure what madam did say, but the meaning was very clear as things usually were in the language of one's servants.

The medical facilities in the district were somewhat sparse and in my view required expansion ahead of frills like mass education, which had little hope of working. The nearest Medical Department doctor was in Ho about 40 miles away from Kpandu. There was a small hospital there which kept the Medical Officer busy, but nevertheless Dr Akwei visited the Kpandu District about once a week and kept a supervisory eye over the dispensaries around the District. There was one of these in Hohoe which was in effect a very small hospital with a few beds with a Dispenser in charge. I had reason to be glad of this hospital under the care of an efficient Dispenser; he should perhaps have been called a Nurse. On one occasion there was an accident just outside my bungalow. I heard a lorry coming up the drive which was unusual after dark. Then there was a loud crash. I looked out down the hill and saw two headlights one above the other. Clearly there was a lorry on its side and I found it was a nasty accident. The lorry had gone over a parapet and landed on its left-hand side. The driver's mate had been thrown out from the left-hand seat and crushed to death, and there was an injured man to be got out of the middle seat; the driver had extricated himself, but he was in a very shocked state, although uninjured. The injured man turned out to be the police sergeant whom the driver was obliging by bringing back to his station. Eventually with the aid of Police Inspector Sanniez and various others who had arrived the back of my pick-up was made into an uncomfortable ambulance and I took the sergeant to hospital in Hohoe over corrugated roads with the inspector acting as attendant in the back. I was very favourably impressed by the efficiency of the staff in Hohoe and happily the sergeant was not seriously hurt and able to return to duty about a week later.

The driver of the lorry was eventually fined £30 – a large sum for him at the time – for careless driving. The case was heard in Ho, as I could not hear it in Kpandu with my knowledge of events. Surprisingly the driver came to thank me after this event for helping him with his problems. To a certain extent I blamed myself for the accident, as I realized the road for which I was responsible was not clearly marked with some white posts. This was done immediately, but interestingly a short time ago in Britain a suggestion I made about some similar marking to a dangerous piece of road was rejected on the grounds that there had not been any reports of accidents. Perhaps I should not have blamed myself too much.

I found Dr Akwei's visits useful in a number of ways as well as enjoying his company. My own health was usually good, but early in my days in Kpandu I felt a little feverish from time to time. Paludrin was the recommended anti-malarial drug at the time and I understood the dosage should be two tablets a week but Dr Akwei advised me that one a day was necessary when living in the bush. By the time I left West Africa the recommended dose was two a day; the malarial parasite had shown its frequent ability to adapt to humanly devised defences. Mosquitoes in Kpandu were often very prevalent as the teak trees planted in the German days formed little cups on the ground, which collected water for breeding in the rainy season. Otherwise, the trees were a fine source of timber which we used for road culverts, buildings and furniture.

I also obtained help from Dr Akwei over another matter. I had received a warning over a bad telephone line from Accra about a local medical student who was said to be returning from Edinburgh after a mental breakdown. As far as I could make out there was some worry because the young man had given his attentions to European ladies on the boat coming back in a manner which made them wonder about his intentions. I made reassuring noises saying that there were very few European ladies in the area and I was quite sure those were quite able to look after themselves. A short time later a very pleasant and inoffensive young man came to see me and my diagnosis of his problem was the same as that of Dr Akwei, who had himself been a student at Edinburgh. He told me the third year was very tough, so I felt sorry for the young man, who without any highly educated family background had probably done well to get as far as he had. As far as ladies were concerned he had probably found the Scottish ones very friendly and did not know that a few British ones in the Gold Coast lived in towns or mining settlements in their own little cocoons.

I did not take the Customs Preventive Service work on the French frontier too seriously, but Buckley the Customs Officer at Dafo fifteen miles away was a friend of mine and my nearest government neighbour. He was always known as Buck and he had a fine body of men under his command. They were mostly ex-servicemen and I had them in mind as useful people in the event of any civil disturbances. After the riots of 1948 we all had a security plan and they figured largely in mine, although never required. On one occasion when I visited Dafo a group of the Preventive Service men were busily engaged digging under the verandah of Buck's swish (a weak mixture of mud and cement) bungalow. The verandah looked to be in imminent danger of collapse. Buck had suddenly found a large ant hill appearing under a wooden pillar; this had been rapidly built by white ants (termites) which could build a hill with remarkable speed. Unfortunately in doing this they had eaten through a wooden pillar which supported the roof. Eventually the versatile Prevention Service men put everything back together again and the white ants went elsewhere.

On another occasion I did a rather foolish thing on leaving Dafo late in the evening. In order to turn my car round I drove it some fifty yards or so beyond the customs post and did a U-turn to face the road for entry into the Gold Coast. Officially I had been into French territory, although the French Customs post was a mile or so away. I found myself confronted by a menacing looking sentry with a rifle. When I stopped I found Buck running out. He explained that the sentry was a Bazzabarimi with a distinguished war record who might have done anything if I had not stopped. The Bazzabarimis made fine soldiers, but Buck explained he was always worried lest they forgot the difference between civil and military duties. They came from French territory lying to the north of the Gold Coast.

Members of the Education Department visited the Kpandu District from time to time. It was part of Jack Bannockie's area of responsibility whilst I was there. He took a robust view on life in general and on education in particular; the idea of getting results from mass education did not appeal to him, or to many members of his department. Unfortunately it had a popular political appeal and it was difficult for any government officer to express in simple and acceptable terms why it would not work. The schools in the Kpandu District were run by the missions on efficient lines, but there were sometimes problems arising from good teachers losing their jobs through following their customary attitude to sexual morality rather than that of their religious denomination. In some ways the Roman Catholic missions adopted a more relaxed view towards these matters and they were happy to marry couples who had lived together and produced children over a period of years. I had great admiration for the Roman Catholic Fathers and Brothers who lived simple lives in the bush. There were a number living in a mission establishment in Kpandu run by Father Van Gaskell, who like many of his church in Togoland was of Dutch nationality. The name of the bishop in charge of the whole area was Holland, but somewhat incongruously he was, I believe, Irish.

I quite often met the Kpandu Fathers on their evening walk when I likewise was taking some exercise in the cooler part of the day. If it happened near my bungalow I sometimes asked them to come up the 28 steps to have a drink. They enjoyed a little drop of whisky and one occasion the bell rang in the town for their evening mass. Far from being disturbed they were rather amused by the lack of a priest to take the mass; they regarded the problem of how one of the Brothers would deal with the matter with some amusement. I loved their humanity as well as admiring their devotion to their religion. My attitude perhaps contrasted with my Anglican upbringing in the inter-war years. The Brothers too were fine men employed to look after buildings and the practical things of life.

As often happened when I was really getting to know the district towards the end of 1948 I had to move. Whilst Tom Hindle had been in charge of the enlarged Ho-Kpandu-Keta District things had proceeded as smoothly as could be expected in the general political turmoil, but now it was time for John Dixon, a substantive Senior District Commissioner to take over; Kpandu was regarded as Tom Hindle's district, so he had to return after handing over. I had to go to Keta from where the DC, John Green, was going on leave. I thought, wrongly as it turned out, that Keta would be my district. I was sorry to leave Kpandu as I was just reaching the point at which I thought I could get to grips with the Native Authorities and Native Courts. Some attention from the government in Accra was given to the Kpandu District owing to the prospect of a visit from the UN Trusteeship Council, but Nkrumah's followers had tended to leave it alone. It was beyond the Volta and protected by some very rough roads.

CHAPTER X

Ewes Outside Togoland

T HE PEOPLE OF THE KETA DISTRICT were Ewes of the
same tribal origins as those with whom I had enjoyed
working in Kpandu. Like the Togolanders they were not attuned to working in large native authorities. There were head
chiefs, but affiliations were loose ones. Togbe Sri lived in Keta
and he was nominally the head of the Anlo tribe. His seat of
authority, such as it was, should have been in Anloga about
ten miles from Keta, but that remained a fishing village with
very independent people; they were liable to riot on a mere
mention of local taxation.

The Keta District was bounded on the east side by French
Togoland with a border which ran north west; the French
capital was Lome, a town by the sea just across the border. The
coastline of the District ran in a general south westerly direction
to the mouth of the Volta River about 40 miles inside the Gold
Coast from the French frontier. Behind the coastal strip there
was a lagoon up to ten miles wide in places. The town of Keta
was on the coastal strip, which was generally not more than
two miles wide. In the rainy season it was often much less than
this; there was at that time a very inconvenient place between
the DC's office and his bungalow where the sea and the lagoon
sometimes met for short periods at high tide. In the west the
District boundary followed the Volta River north westwards
for about forty miles. The northern boundary was the old
German boundary between Togoland and the Gold Coast; it
was sixty miles due east to the French frontier. Most of the
economic activity was along the coastline with many fishing
villages and settlements; coconut palms also provided the people
living there with a source of income. Smuggling to and from
French territory by canoe was another occupation for fishermen.
Smuggling was never taken very seriously by the administration
either side of the border; during my days in Keta wines and
cigarettes came into the district and bicycles and other commodities went out. I remember one day when a man came to
see me and asked with a very serious face whether I had heard
about the canoe accident. I had not heard about it and I asked

A typical beach scene. *Canham Collection* published by kind permission of Cambridge University Library.

whether anyone was drowned; he replied 'No, but twelve bicycles were lost'.

The town of Keta developed around an old Dutch and later Danish trading centre. The people opposed the establishment of a foreign settlement, but eventually the Danes after a successful military campaign built a fort in 1784. This was subsequently restored in 1847 shortly before the Danes sold it with other Gold Coast possessions to the British in 1850. It was much later put to various uses including housing a prison and providing an office for the DC.

There was not much economic activity on the infertile hinterland behind the lagoon, but there were a large number of fishing and farming settlements along the banks of the Volta and farming settlements along the road running north west near the French frontier through Djoje (pronounced Jo-jay) into the Ho District. Beyond the Volta River there was the Ada District, which was administered in my time as part of the Keta District. Before Takoradi Harbour was built Ada was an important port, but it had been in decline for some twenty years. The younger people had mostly left and the scene in the town was often a deserted one. It came to life once a month when I held court there; then gathering at the court house was a social occasion. The cases were mostly dull ones about indebtedness. Land disputes were another serious occupation, but DCs outside the Northern Territories were not permitted to become concerned with litigation over these matters.

When I went to Keta at the end of 1948 the political situation in the country was one of great uncertainty. It was the middle of the next year before Nkrumah formed the CPP as a break-away party, but he was already the dominant personality; this became clear in Keta whilst I was there. There was a general feeling amongst DCs that the Governor, Sir Gerald Creasy, was not in control of affairs. We were used in the Districts to having little contact with the Governor, but we liked to feel he was there and in control. In fairness to Sir Gerald it must be said that the Colonial Office and the Watson Commission had limited his scope for governing. He had to set up a Committee to consider the constitution, which he did under Mr Justice (later Sir Henley) Coussey. The country was, therefore, inevitably in an interim phase.

There were three other senior government officers in Keta as well as the DC, representing the Police, Medical and Public Works Departments. Peter Jelacsics (pronounced Jel-ace-ics) was in charge of the police. He was a very efficient police officer with a sense of humour that I found refreshing when he made one of his frequent visits to my office in the morning. His name hardly surprisingly caused some difficulty to the local people and on different occasions he brought me envelopes addressed to Mr J. Six and Mr Jelly for Six.

Maurice Brown was the medical officer. Like most of his kind he held strong views on how medical services should be run, but I found him a very pleasant person. He was interested in sailing and I went out with him on the Keta lagoon, but sailing there was not a great success as much time was spent on sandbanks and a certain amount of wading was necessary. On one occasion Maurice showed great interest in some snails and said he wondered whether those were the snails which were hosts to the bilharzia parasite. This disease happily was not very common in the Gold Coast unlike the Nile valley. It was caused by a schistosome, which had a life cycle from the human bladder through water into some kind of snail and then back into the water to invade the human body through the legs or other exposed skin. I was happy to leave the snails behind as perhaps best left undisturbed.

Small government stations always had a certain number of feuds between the incumbents of various offices; most of these were not serious. Unfortunately, there was quite an intense one between Maurice Brown and Peter Jelacsics. I thought I would try asking them both to dinner and after a somewhat stormy evening I decided it had not been a good idea. However, about a week later Peter had a nasty attack of malaria and after that they were friends, as Maurice went to great trouble in treating him.

The oldest government inhabitant of Keta was Harry Peters of the Public Works Department, who with his wife, Nan, had spent some years in Keta. They were a friendly couple and Nan regarded herself as 'in loco parentis' to young thirty-year-olds like me. Harry was a short time from retirement and followed a set routine. He was determined to keep his old pre-war Chevrolet (they were well-made cars) going until his retirement. He used to proceed to his office with great regularity at 8.40 a.m. and I used to know when this was happening, as there were some women working on cracking stones for building works in the prison. Until 8.35 a.m. there was the intermittent sound of stones being cracked, but by 8.40 a.m. the whole of the old fort resounded to the beating of hammers. There was a short inspection by Harry and then the noise returned to its inter-mittent nature after a short rest on his departure. I did not in any way interfere with this well established custom, but I did try to get Harry to remove dangerous palms from hanging over the road between Keta and the French frontier. I did not achieve any success. Sadly Harry's wife died shortly after he retired, but I was very happy to meet him again when he returned to the Gold Coast to take on the role of looking after ancient monuments.

I was very well served by the clerks in the office in Keta, but special mention must be made of the office messenger, Banga (sic) Acolatse. There were a number of Acolatses in Keta, mostly in jobs of some substance, but Banga was an apparently unambitious one. He had a very wide range of friends and acquaintances and he had much local knowledge about people in Keta; he liked to feel he had the ear of the DC. As well as friends there were a few people he did not like and he was not slow to warn against them. In my case this included a lady who was reported to have been the 'friend' of one or two DC predecessors. Banga had been in the battalion of the Gold Coast Regiment to which I belonged for a short time in 1940. When the battalion was in the Gambia after I had left it he distinguished himself by finding a deserter and bringing him back. He had hived up in a local brothel and Banga claimed and obtained expenses of ten shillings (50p) which he had incurred in the establishment whilst finding the missing soldier.

Both the French and the British governments had exchange controls in the late nineteen forties, but I do not think anyone in Keta outside the bank knew how they worked. As far as government officers were concerned the customary system was to ask the DC how to acquire some francs. Banga then played an important part in the process in exchanging pounds for francs at a very favourable rate. I never knew how far his operations on the currency market accounted for his apparent lack of ambition, as he was an intelligent man. Another Acolatse, Charles, was a judge who became a friend later on, but I never liked to ask him whether he was related to Banga.

Liaison with the French played an important part in the job of the DC, Keta. There was a mutual interest of British and French Governments in UN Trusteeship, so efforts were made to bring about closer co-operation across the border. Liaison was usually between the Secretariat in Accra and their counterparts in Lome the headquarters of the French Togoland government. Mike Ensor on the British side and Monsieur Doz on the French side were normally responsible for liaison, but occasionally it was necessary to ask the DC Keta to visit the French, as he was near at hand and usually associated socially with the French. I was somewhat handicapped in not having advanced beyond Higher Certificate schoolboy French, although with practice much came back to me. On one occasion I spent the night at the Aflao rest house just by the border in order to go to a morning meeting in the French headquarters in Lome and I found myself looking at a beautiful sunrise behind the waves greeting the morning in French. I was somewhat worried about how far the meeting would be conducted in English or a mixture of French and English; fortunately my fears were groundless, as the faithful Monsieur Doz was present and he was very fluent in English. After the meeting he took me for a glass of beer with his usual hospitality.

My arrival in Keta was not long before Christmas 1948 and the New Year of 1949 and there was some Anglo-French celebration particularly over the New Year on the French side. Champagne seemed to be plentiful and not very expensive. I remember one occasion on which Bishop Holland, who was head of the Roman Catholic church in the area, gave me the very good advice at a social gathering that another glass of champagne would improve my French. The bishop was a charming man with whom I played tennis. In his younger days he must have been a good player and I had difficulty in giving him a game, despite being his junior in age by at least 20 years.

The French administrative system had many similarities to our own and in general revolved around the Commandant de Cercle, who was in a similar position to a DC. The French were very keen on village schools and village dispensaries. There were similarities here, but they seemed to do more in the way of dispensaries and small hospitals, although this impression may have arisen solely from better markings for such places. French theories on government were quite different from British ones in that they believed in teaching Africans in French ways rather than trying to develop their own institutions. Their vision for the future was one of a large part of Africa becoming part of a greater France. Britain on the other hand saw the future in terms of each African country running its own affairs in association with Britain; we did of course see this only as a long term development. Our differences with African politicians were largely based on timing. Their demand was for self-government now, whereas our thinking was in favour of a much slower process towards self-government when they were ready for it. The French view likewise was a long term one, as educating Africans into becoming like Frenchmen was inevitably something which would take generations; like us they had politicians with different ideas on timing.

The problems of local government in the Keta District were similar to those in Togoland further north. There was more money in the Keta District, but an equally great reluctance to part with it and the problem of collecting a local rate (a poll tax) was similar. It was not a matter over which Togbe Sri had much control although we spent hours discussing it. From time to time a messenger from Togbe would come into my office in the morning and say Togbe would be very pleased if I would call to see him on my way home at lunchtime. Drinking most of a bottle of champagne was an inevitable adjunct of the meeting followed by the abandonment of work for the afternoon. As a result of these meetings it was agreed that my scheme of beginning to try to collect the rate in the Djoje area would be adopted. This was contrary to the view of John Dixon, my Senior District Commissioner, who thought we ought to start in Anloga ten miles from Keta which was traditionally Togbe's town and the hard core of resistance. Happily John Dixon left me largely to my own devices in a very friendly way so we began in Djoje. Later when Nkrumah had become Chief Minister it was decreed that Anloga should be tackled. This led to my friend Alan Cowley, who was DC at the time, getting stabbed for his trouble in the course of a riot. Fortunately, he was successfully taken out of the village and received medical attention soon enough to save his life.

I cannot claim much success in Djoje before I left the District, but it was a place in which something useful could be seen to be happening. Before my arrival in Keta the Water Supply Department had decided Djoje would be a suitable place for a deep borehole. A contract was made with the Balakani Black Sea Oil Company, who sent a driller by the name of Rigold. He was a well qualified and well cultured man. He had learnt his mining engineering at the Camborne School of Mines and I found him most interesting. He occupied the rest house in Djoje and made me most welcome whenever I visited him. His cook always produced a good meal and the Driller had some knowledge of cooking himself. Amongst other things he explained the improvement brought about in soup by the addition of a little sherry. His drilling work was done by the slow process of dropping a heavy bit onto the ground and gradually going down in that way. He explained that a rotary drill would be no good as it would be likely to penetrate a layer of water and simply make a way through an impervious clay into the earth below. The problem with the implement he was using was to keep it straight. If the bit got out of line there was a danger it would get stuck down the hole; Driller Rigold delighted in telling me how one of his predecessors in the Northern Territories had left his tools down a hole and gone home to the UK.

When working on his own in Djoje the Driller was very strict with himself in avoiding alcohol. He was, however, always pleased to have a visitor to relieve him of this well disciplined rule and at week-ends he used often to betake himself to the Hotel du Golfe in Lome. After one such visit I had to exercise some international diplomacy with the hotel manager, as the Driller had been expelled from the hotel and told not to come back. On the previous Saturday night he had been sitting at the bar and caught hold of the bar rail whilst emphasizing a point; he leant backwards and his weight was such that the bamboo structure collapsed and down came the bar, bottles, glasses, Driller and all. Fortunately, nobody was hurt at all seriously, but the hotel manager was somewhat displeased when he came upon the scene of devastation. Happily my later visit together with the Driller settled everything amicably on payment of some compensation and a number of handshakes. Eventually in Djoje the Driller struck water, but I had left the District, so I could not develop my theme of payment of rates as a quid pro quo for water.

The Hotel du Golfe was a social asset for the DC and others living in Keta. The French were very hospitable and I remember staying in a French household for a night when my hostess insisted that as an Englishman I must have bacon and egg for breakfast – not actually my custom in West Africa. The French ladies at the Hotel du Golfe when I went there were very patient in helping me to speak French. I appreciated this, but I was less happy with my dancing lessons. I could cope quite easily with waltzes and foxtrots, but nearly every other dance seemed to be a tango; I think both my first and my last tango were in Lome.

Nkrumah brought Keta into the mainstream of national politics whilst I was there. He made a number of visits and on the first made his usual strong impression with his confident and outgoing personality. As DC I had to report this event to the Secretariat in Accra typed by my own hands with copies to others in the normal chain of communications such as my Senior DC. In the report I mentioned that two well respected African managers Newlands and Baeta of UAC (United Africa Company) accompanied Nkrumah on a visit to Lome. This did not surprise me although I knew Newlands and Baeta well as friends. They were prominent in the All Ewe Movement and might have been expected to be somewhat opposed to a politician with a strong Gold Coast orientation. However, Nkrumah coming as he did from Nzima at the opposite side of the country probably needed some local help from such persons in meeting people in Lome. From this point of view it would have been difficult to refuse to go. There was, however,

Paul with Kayah

surprise in the Secretariat and I was rung up by one Alan Kerr. I should perhaps explain that there were by coincidence two persons named Alan Kerr in the Administration in the Gold Coast; there the similarity ended. One was a DC who pronounced his name as spelt and the other was a Secretariat officer who pronounced his name as Carr. It was the latter who rang me and in the course of a conversation couched in terms designed to maintain security obviously doubted my report. It was all part of a scepticism amongst staff at almost any headquarters doubting information which does not fit in with their previously conceived ideas. Many years earlier in world history Galileo had his difficulties with the Pope.

Nkrumah's interest in Keta brought national politics into

Paul on a visit to his village of Ayinasi

the area. A campaign began of shouting self-government at me as DC and other people with white faces; this lasted until a short time after I had left Keta. It was not in any way threatening, but it is unpleasant to feel unwanted. The session of the Coussey Committee on Constitutional Reform held in Keta gave rise to a crescendo in the campaign and after a brief visit to the sitting of the Committee to make sure they had all the facilities they needed I found my car covered with the letters SG. The wooden back to the Dodge Pick-up made a perfect blackboard for this activity. Fortunately only chalk was used, so it was easily cleaned off. I found the shouting of self-government or SG for short did not happen if I was walking as I frequently did around the town in the evening. There was just one occasion when a young lad shouted from an alleyway and tried to hide when I turned towards him. I asked him who he was and he proudly replied 'I am a Standard 7 schoolboy'. I thought it fair to ask the lad who had reached the highest standard of education below the secondary level what he meant by self-government. He replied 'It is government for yourself; you do what you like'. After I pointed out that he might find things were not quite like that we both laughed and I moved on to receive my usual friendly greetings from people in the town. I found it reassuring after the shouts I received when travelling by car.

My African friends wisely advised me to take no notice of this
and I tried to appear to have deaf ears.

My sojourn in Keta was cut short by the frequent practice of
'general post' when someone went on leave. Tom Hindle was
going on leave from Kpandu and John Dixon wanted me back
in Togoland in the middle of 1949 to help preparations for the
UN Mission visit at the end of year, so I had to leave the sea
and return to the more hilly country around Kpandu. As usual
there was no trouble over moving as one's servants were very
efficient at this. My domestic staffing had undergone a change
in Keta. My steward boy, Kabba, took to drink in Keta and
became increasingly incompetent. After I sent him out of the
house one evening when he was more drunk than usual he told
me next morning that I had sacked him and he was going.
With some relief I agreed with his interpretation and filled in
his steward's licence book with as little comment as possible.
The whole affair had a happy outcome for me, as I was able
to take on Paul Kweku, who remained with me for the rest of

Below: A group in
Ayinasi

Above: Another
scene in Ayinasi

Bortey doing
Sunday morning
maintenance

my time in the Gold Coast. When Faith joined me on my next tour Paul was well liked by her and we were both in touch with Paul by letter until he died in 1992.

Another person who joined my establishment shortly after I left Keta and also stayed with me for the rest of my time was Silas Bortey, a mechanic who later became a driver. In Keta most people living in the government bungalows employed 'Kofi Fitter' to carry out car maintenance on Sunday mornings. I never knew Kofi's real name, but he was known to everyone as Kofi Fitter. He had an army of fitter's mates of whom Bortey was the senior and he suggested that when I went to Kpandu I should take Bortey with me. I refused the offer at the time, but when something went wrong soon after my arrival in Kpandu I sent for Bortey and he stayed. Paul and Bortey thus became my permanent staff. Paul became cook-steward assisted by 'small boys' mostly of his choosing. Bortey was most successful at keeping me out of any major mechanical trouble and I had few bills from car workshops.

CHAPTER XI

Sir Charles Arden-Clarke

IN AUGUST 1949 Sir Charles Arden-Clarke took over as Governor; this was more than a year after Sir Gerald Creasy had left. At the time the feeling was that there had not been a Governor in charge of the situation since Sir Alan Burns left two years earlier. This made an ideal situation for politicians such as Kwame Nkrumah to develop their influence. Sir Charles visited Togoland fairly soon after becoming Governor. His visit to Kpandu made two things clear to me. First, we had someone who was going to be properly in charge of the situation. Second, we were going to have to make rapid progress towards self-government, if we were to avoid serious trouble and a general loss of good-will in the country. I took Sir Charles around the government station in Kpandu on the evening of his arrival. He asked how much a new rest house had cost. This was a slightly embarrassing question as we had £200 allocated to the district for this, but by various means including the use of prison labour I had managed to build something rather better than £200 could buy. I should not have worried as he was well acquainted with the ways of district administration from his days in Northern Nigeria. I was also amused by his reaction when I asked him if he would like to see inside the prison. He looked at his watch, which was rapidly approaching 6.0 p.m., and said 'I think I have seen enough prisons in my time'. It was obviously time for a drink.

We had some heavy rains shortly before the Governor's visit, so I thought there was a danger that one of the roads chosen for him would be impassable. About a week before he was due to arrive I suggested to John Dixon, my SDC, that the Governor should take a slightly longer route. John expressed horror at the idea of diverting the Governor, and was unimpressed by my argument that a Governor with Nigerian experience would understand the problem of heavy rains, but might well be annoyed if he became stuck en route to Kpandu. There we left the matter after a telephone conversation at about 8.00 a.m. At noon I made my customary journey up the 28 steps to the bungalow and I was seated with my footstool in place and a cold glass of beer awaiting consumption when a car drew up. On going to see who was the visitor I found Morton Weatherburn had been despatched from Ho by John to give me some help having been told I was absolutely overwhelmed with work. I had in fact been working since about 7.00 a.m., but Morton and I laughed at the difference between the picture painted by John and what he found on arrival in Kpandu. Needless to say another bottle of beer was quickly brought so that we could discuss the matter properly and after some lunch Morton went to examine the scene. He closed the road until the Governor's arrival and had a gang of road labourers standing by in case the Governor's car required a shove. Happily His Excellency did not need any shoving.

On my return to the Kpandu District the situation was less tranquil than formerly. Political influences from Kwame Nkrumah and the Togo Union, particularly the former, were making themselves felt. The general message from Nkrumah was one of opposing anything supported by the Colonial Government. There was fertile ground in encouraging refusal to pay rates. A small place, Likpe Mate, a short distance from Hohoe was a centre of opposition stirred up by one Kwesi Minta, who was dubbed the Nkrumah of Likpe. He caused annoyance to the Native Authority in Hohoe, which wanted to go and arrest him and bring him before the Native Court. I discouraged this action, as I was too familiar with the story of NA Policemen ill trained and badly equipped trying to arrest people and failing. There were too many incidents reported with the colourful phrase 'they took to their heels'. I promised to go to Likpe, but before I had time to do this I received a triumphant telephone call from Hohoe saying Kwesi Minta had been arrested in the town. I knew this meant that trouble was probable, so I told the caller not to do anything until I arrived; before leaving I made sure that the Government Police in Hohoe knew what was happening.

On arrival in Hohoe I was most impressed by the way the Police had handled the situation. There were about a dozen lorries halted on the Likpe road on the outskirts of the town. They had been told to stay there by one Escort Police Sergeant. He was a fine figure of a Northern Territories man looking very smart in appearance and wearing a number of war ribbons; nobody questioned his authority. Outside the courthouse there was an Escort Constable who was disregarding the principle of open court and stopping people going in. I left him to carry on and, contrary to good judicial practice, I told the court to call the case and grant bail as soon as possible. This was duly done and the cavalcade of lorries returned in triumph to Likpe. It was a day on which everyone could claim victory; I include myself, as there was not a riot. The case against Kwesi Minta was quietly dropped through a number of adjournments, but he did not give much more trouble.

In the Buem Native Authority with headquarters in Jasikan in the North of the District there was a better record of paying the rate than elsewhere, but unfortunately the NA became too ambitious; it decided that women should also be taxed. From the point of view of getting money from people making it the principle was sound, but I was not in the District when the resolution was passed and I did not know how much preparation there had been. The Buem State was one in which some Akan customs prevailed so I said I would go and talk to the Queen Mothers in Borada, a village a few miles from Jasikan. I expected to meet about half a dozen ladies for a friendly chat, but when I arrived I found a large meeting of around two hundred. When I explained that I had not come to address a large meeting, but just to meet the Queen Mothers, I was given an indignant reply – 'We are all Queen Mothers'. Opposition to paying tax was voiced in the words 'Our grandmothers never paid tax and we will not pay tax'. I tried to point out some improvements since the days of their grandmothers like the motorable road from Jasikan and the medical clinic in Jasikan. This was of no avail and they gradually became more angry so I decided to leave with what dignity, if any, that I could muster. When I approached the area of the gathering in my car on the way out of the village I found they had assembled in the road, but they divided their ranks and showered the car with gravel. I was unharmed, but my cook, Paul Kweku, in the back of the car got some gravel in his eye; happily this was efficiently removed by the nurse in the clinic in Jasikan. For my part I could only contemplate and try to learn from a series of mistakes; the last of these was parking my car facing in the wrong direction.

A much more unpleasant event occurred in Hohoe when a mentally deranged Fulani herdsman went into a school and attacked children and their teacher with a cutlass. Several children were killed and injured and the teacher was very badly lacerated. The man had apparently complained earlier that the children were throwing stones at his cows. I arrived in the town from Jasikan where I had spent the night at about 9.0 a. m. in the morning on the way back to Kpandu. Not knowing what had happened I had hoped to make one or two calls and then go on my way, but instead I had to try to pacify the town. The first indication that something was wrong came from seeing a man carrying a gun running back towards the Zongo which contained the Hausa community. It was quite common to see people carrying guns, but the fact that he was running seemed strange. It was very difficult to find out what had happened. There were groups of young men shouting and waving their arms and women weeping. There happened to be a reporter of the Gold Coast Express in the town and I seized upon him to help me unravel what had happened. The Fulani man had been disarmed by an act of great bravery by his own Chief to whom he had handed his cutlass. Most of the injured had been conveyed to the small hospital, which was surrounded by a large crowd; the police had taken the Fulani into custody. The needs now were to get medical aid for the injured, as the hospital did not have a doctor in charge, and to try to calm the situation.

There was little I could do towards re-establishing tranquillity apart from just walking around in the streets and in this I was helped in talking to people by using the Express reporter as an interpreter. He had of course great pleasure in reporting this in his paper, but I was happy to find he gave a much more favourable report of my action as DC than was common at the time. At one stage I found myself surrounded by a group of angry young men who were interpreting the happenings as a plot by the Zongo people against the Ewe townsfolk. They even went so far as to suggest that there were Hausamen from the Zongo in the bush ready to attack the town. Clutching at a proverbial straw I suggested that they would do better to go to bush and see for themselves that this was not happening; I thought the Zongo people were in fact all in their own quarters somewhat fearful of what might happen. I realized, however, soon after I had made the remark that there could have been an unfortunate Hausaman in the bush not knowing anything about the affair who might have been attacked. In fact of course they had no intention of moving out of town and the situation gradually calmed itself.

I spoke to Amable, the Superintendent of Police in Ho by telephone, as soon as I could do so and he decided to send for the Mobile Force from Accra. A lorry load of these duly arrived in the evening when the situation had calmed, but they had to hurry back to Accra on the next day, as Nkrumah was stirring up some trouble there. By that time it was all quiet with business as usual in Hohoe. Getting a doctor was a greater worry, as the medical officer in Ho was unable to leave his hospital there. However, I managed to get a young newly qualified privately practising African doctor from Kadjebi in the north of the District. When he came he was very impresssed by the work done by the hospital staff. I asked him to send me a bill for his services, which I promised to submit to the Government. He would not have anything to do with this idea, saying that he was glad to be able to help people when they were in trouble and he did not want any payment. When reporting the incident John Dixon was kind enough to say that I had handled it well. It was really a case of doing nothing in particular apart from being there, and letting the storm blow itself out.

There was also a lighter side of life in the Kpandu District. One day I had a visit from a man who said he had trouble in keeping his son in order. He said he had heard that there was a good school for such boys in Winneba and asked whether I could arrange for his son to go there. The good school was a recently opened Borstal Institution. It was difficult to explain that the boy would have to put a brick through a window in my office in order to qualify and then only if the magistrate thought fit.

The prison also continued to provide a source of amusement from time to time. On a Saturday afternoon when I was enjoying the half day we had off work there was a noisy drumming from the prison. When I enquired what was happening I was told that the prisoners were practising for the Christmas party. This was some months ahead and I did not think it right that prisoners supposedly being punished should disturb the peace of a Saturday afternoon, so I ordered a cessation of this activity. On a later occasion when I visited the prison I saw a group of prisoners sitting around in a circle making beating gestures in the air. When I asked what they were doing the answer was 'They are doing silent practice'. I relented in respect of my previous instruction by saying that I did not mind drumming at reasonable hours in the evening, but not on a Saturday afternoon.

Another very pleasant side of life in Kpandu was having some very good friends. Relationships within the Administrative Service were very good. I did not always agree with John Dixon, the Senior District Commissioner, but our disagreements were always on a very amicable basis; our problems were always quite easily resolved sometimes with the aid of a drink in the evening. Others with whom I enjoyed lasting friendships were Tom Hindle, Morton Weatherburn and David Heaton. David had taken over from me in Keta and for some reason the shouting of self-government died down. I do not know whether David was more awe inspiring to the populace or thought to be kinder; it is more likely that they just became tired of it.

There was a visit from the Gold Coast Film Unit, which came to make a film of one of the Mass Education rallies. Unfortunately they came during the rainy season and could not do much filming. I particularly remember the camera man, George Noble, who was a most jovial character and quite unworried by the frustration of overcast skies which marked their visit. Their Director was a much more serious character and decided to inspect his servants' latrines. Needless to say these left much to be desired and were the subject of a complaint to me as DC. It was an area I preferred to leave to look after itself, but a working party of prisoners was duly organized.

There was a tendency amongst DCs to be somewhat cynical about mass education and similar schemes. This was not because the idea was thought bad, but there seemed to be a

lack of provision for continuity in supervision. Alec Dickson
had great faith in the advantages of setting something going
but he was too optimistic in this. Personally I saw roads and
bridges, particularly the latter, as ways forward. Bridges and
culverts were important as they provided an incentive amongst
the local people to keep the road open at least in the dry
season. In Kpandu and Togoland in general there were useful
tradesmen, such as carpenters and mechanics. In Kpandu there
was a carpenters workshop on the Government premises run
by Ephraim Attoh, who was equally at home constructing a
wooden culvert and making a table for a rest house. I regarded
furniture for rest houses as important if people were to be
encouraged to visit places in the bush. Some people who
had not been equipped by tropical outfitters down to the
last detail found sleeping on a camp bed with nothing else
to sit on somewhat discouraging. Another craft which flourished in Kpandu was ivory carving in a business run by an
elderly carver, who also had a finger in the local political
pie.

I had hoped that when Tom Hindle returned from leave at
the end of November, 1949, I should be able to go on leave in
time for Christmas with my family. However, John Dixon
wrote to Sutherland as Acting Chief Commissioner asking for

Kpandu carpenters

more staff to cover the visit of the UN Mission. The reply came saying simply 'Dennis will have to extend his tour'. I was perhaps stupidly very annoyed by the tone and nature of the reply, as it would have been so much easier and nicer to say that I should be asked to do so. In that event refusing to do so would have been far from my thoughts, whereas having completed my eighteen months without a day off I could have gone to the medical officer and obtained a recommendation that I should be sent on leave. The effect of getting annoyed was not a good one as I immediately proceeded to run up a high temperature and feel very poorly for 24 hours. Anne Hindle (Tom's wife) used to tell Tom not to get himself worked up as it was bad for his parasites; I reckoned I had proved her theory and admired the medical perspicacity of a former nursing sister.

After handing over the Kpandu District to Tom Hindle I took up residence in Ho, where I could perhaps be described as a DC without portfolio. However, there was plenty to do before the UN Mission arrived and I enjoyed helping John Dixon in this. Later I wrote the report for the Southern part of Togoland for Mike Ensor to coordinate with the Northern part for the UN Trusteeship Council.

The UN Mission had four members and a number of secretaries and advisers. The chairman was a dour Iraqi and he was assisted by an ebullient American, a Mexican and a Belgian. The Mexican kept reiterating how many days it was since he left his newly married wife. I remember seventeen days being mentioned and avoiding saying that it was over seventeen months since I left my family; it would have been regarded as unimportant. The Belgian, Clayes Bouert, had been a provincial governor in the Belgian Congo and he had a good understanding of what he was seeing. I sat next to him at dinner one evening and he said he was surprised how much freedom the Africans enjoyed. He had seen a demonstration with placards saying 'We want water', 'We want hospitals', 'We want schools' and similar things. He went on to say he thought we allowed too much freedom. Some years later I saw the effects of less freedom when the Belgians left the Congo in chaos.

The year 1950 began with Kwame Nkrumah's campaign of Positive Action for Self Government. The general idea was to paralyse the country with strikes and demonstrations. Emergency legislation was passed to deal with the situation and the police were well organized for public disorder. The police carried long batons and were not armed with rifles, but unfortunately two policemen were killed in Accra by stab wounds when dispersing a mob. Nkrumah and other leaders who incited mobs and strikes were gaoled for varying periods after the action was over. There was not much trouble outside Accra where the local press took a surprisingly impartial line. There was criticism of the government, but there was a clear respect for the firm line taken. One paper had an amusing headline 'The ruler and the ruled'. A crowd in Accra went to the DC's office demanding to see the DC, but Lindsay Britton was out elsewhere at the scene of some action. His wife, a redoubtable Polish lady, had been helping in the office during the emergency, so she decided to go out wielding a ruler above her head and tell the assembled populace to go away, as the DC was not there. They meekly went away and gave rise to the remarks in the newspaper.

Positive Action for Self Government subsided fairly rapidly after Nkrumah and others were arrested and the mobs were firmly under control. It was not as Nkrumah probably hoped a repeat of the rioting of 1948. There were more policemen on the streets and in mobile patrols; there was no shooting. The lack of use of firearms was important, as their use would have resulted in a great loss of public support from those without strong political feelings.

I spent another six weeks in Ho writing part of the Togoland report. One day I suddenly found myself alone in the office as everyone had rushed out, making me wonder whether the place was on fire or collapsing. I could not see or hear anything suggesting imminent danger, but on looking over the verandah in the distance I saw a deer. This was being pursued by all the office staff and others from elsewhere. The result was a victory for the deer with its much greater speed, but it was customary for the sighting of a deer to lead to a vain chase. About a quarter of an hour later normal working was resumed.

Early in March I went to Takoradi to join the post-war Elder Dempster ship, *Accra*, which replaced the one sunk during the war. I was slightly less penurious than usual at the end of a tour, as the devaluation of the pound against the dollar resulted in being able to sell my Dodge Pick-up for very little less than I had paid at the beginning of the tour. I had bought it as usual with the aid of a Government loan, but I was able to return that and depart with a balance in my favour. The finances of members of the Colonial Service in the Gold Coast tended to revolve around car loans with favourable repayment conditions, but negative equity although the term was not in use was unfortunately by no means unknown.

When aboard the *Accra* I found I was travelling with two DCs from the Northern Territories, Tony Townsend and Gerrard Charles. I enjoyed many years of friendship with Tony stretching into our retirement from the Colonial Service, but sadly Gerrard died a few years later as a result of a virus infection contracted in the Gold Coast. Both in their service in the North had had much less interference from national politicians and the patrician Muslim society was continuing much as it always had been. I found this interesting, but Tony always took a great interest in what other people were doing and he always showed great consideration for other people. Our discussions may have influenced him in deciding to read for the Bar. He was called to the Bar some years later and founded a successful practice after retirement from the Colonial Service; unlike me he was able to spend time not earning much money, as he was unmarried. He set this right later and married Suzanne, a colleague at the Bar. She bore him three children in fairly rapid succession, but sadly Tony died when they were just beginning on their careers.

Faith and I spent my leave at the same cottage as we had rented on my previous leave. It was a few miles from Oxford and called Old Cottage; our married life in England had been in a number of old cottages; the other two went by the names of Myrtle Cottage and Grey Cottage. We had some lengthy discussions about the future, as being a family for leave only was unsatisfactory from every point of view. It was difficult to envisage any suitable alternative to the Colonial Service, but before coming on leave I had applied to transfer to the Judiciary as a District Magistrate. One advantage of such a move would have been being situated in a town with more amenities and medical care for family life with children. Furthermore there were more opportunities for transfers to other colonies with a more healthy climate. My life as a DC had certainly been interesting and with substantial responsibilities, but it seemed to me that political influences would greatly detract from the nature of the job in the future. I realized that much magisterial work would be routine and boring, but on the other hand there would always be some interesting cases. Furthermore, having done one's best in hearing a case there was some finality in that you did not have to be concerned with the matter further; there could be an appeal, but then a higher court would have to deal with it and dispose of the case.

Another matter with which Faith and I were concerned during a busy leave was schooling for Nigel. We decided we should send him to a boarding school when he reached the age of eight in 1952, so finding a suitable school was a necessary task. Day school education was only possible as long as we accepted being separated and keeping two homes; it would have been an unhappy situation and impracticable on the grounds of expense.

Towards the end of my leave events took an unexpected turn regarding my future in the Gold Coast. My application to become a District Magistrate reached deadlock between the Administration and the Judiciary. The former would not let me go on secondment and the latter would not have me except on a secondment in the first instance. Events in the Colony Administration had also taken an unexpected turn in that Donald Sutherland did not succeed Sir Thorlief Mangin on his retirement, as he went to Accra to become a Permanent Secretary in one of the new ministries to be formed after the elections. In the process of several changes Johnny Loveridge became Chief Commissioner of the Colony. This was greatly welcomed by members of that Administration including myself. To my surprise I was asked to take up the job of Judicial Adviser in Cape Coast under Colin Russell, the newly appointed Senior Judicial Adviser. The job of Judicial Adviser was intended to cover the control and development of native courts; during Johnny Loveridge's time in the post it had been developed in many other interesting directions, such as giving legal advice to District Commissioners. From a work point of view the chain of events affecting me were wholly welcome and the next five years gave me the most interesting work I had in the Colonial Service, or indeed after I left it. There was still the disadvantage of family separations, but at least Faith was able to be with me for part of each of the succeeding tours in West Africa.

CHAPTER XII

The Final Phase Begins

T HE YEAR 1950 saw the beginning of the final colonial phase in the Gold Coast, although Nkrumah and some of his associates were in prison. Preparations for elections early in the next year were pressed forward; there was much doubt about whether Nkrumah's CPP would take part, or how far they would have support in the country. The official CPP line was that the whole proposed constitution was fraudulent. As far as I was concerned the year 1950, likewise, marked the beginning of the final and most interesting phase of my colonial career.

I arrived in Cape Coast to find I was working in the office next to Colin Russell, the SJA. The office also served as a small library and unlike the other offices it did not have a through draught of air from the sea breeze, but I soon made myself quite comfortable with the aid of the fan. Colin gave me an outline of the job in a clear-cut manner and left me to carry on and made himself readily available if I wanted any help. It is the way I have always found it best for learning a job; I have learnt much since that time about the theory of induction and training but for me the simple system is best. One subject on which I remember seeking Colin's advice was how to deal with questions sometimes asked by DCs engaged upon hearing a case in court which they found tricky. It was of course in theory wrong to influence DCs in their magisterial capacity. Colin simply said I usually tell them enough to keep them out of trouble; this I found a remark of infinite wisdom in many fields. I did not have the advantage of Colin's help for very long, as he became heavily engaged in preparations for the elections planned for early in 1951. Amongst other things this involved him in long telephone calls to Michael Gass who was coordinating plans in the Secretariat in Accra. Both Colin and Michael were keen bird watchers and their somewhat heavy conversations about registrations for elections usually ended with remarks about bird sightings like 'Where did you see that, was it a spotted one?'

Chatterings on the telephone to friends were always enjoyable however worrying any situation might be. There were times when the manually operated exchanges did not work very well, but on the whole by standards of the nineteen fifties the telephone system was very good. There were some hard-working linesmen who tried to keep the lines connected whatever the weather. They used to call each other 'lineman' and conversations were sometimes inadvertently interrupted by remarks like 'lineman can you hear me?'. In the Cape Coast office exchange we had two girls who took turns to operate it. These were Susie, who was a shy girl of petite build and Margery, who was podgy and by no means shy. We had an inspection by a senior African telephone exchange supervisor and she came to talk to Colin and me about how the girls were working. We said Susie was very quick and good at her work, but Margery was more lethargic. She asked us whether that was the one who had the baby last year. On being told this was the case she said 'No wonder. I don't think we should give these girls all this maternity leave – not every year'. I do not remember Margery having any more maternity leave whilst I was in Cape Coast; I do not know what advice she had been given by her supervisor.

I was very happy to have the job concerned with Native Courts, as I thought – wrongly as it turned out – that there was a chance of setting up a system of local courts based upon panels of local justices similar to the magistrates courts in Britain. One thing we should have done was to change the name to local courts, but at the time I do not think anyone regarded the term 'native' as derogatory in this context. It should not of course be a derogatory term, but custom and practice have led to it being so, although I for one am very happy to be called a native of Dorset. In the case of Native Courts the term was also too closely associated with Native Authorities largely based upon the old chiefly system; we were trying to break away from that and a change of name for the courts might have helped greatly.

Early in my days as a Judicial Adviser Johnny Loveridge set me the task of analysing what would be the effects of transferring the Krachi District from the Northern Territories to the Colony with which it was considered to have more affinities. It was also somewhat remote from Tamale from where the Northern Territories were administered. This was also the case in so far as Cape Coast was concerned, but there were various intermediary centres of enlarged districts. Carrying out an analysis of the legal effects of such a change was a very useful exercise from my point of view as it was necessary to go through all the Gold Coast legislation systematically moving from each Ordinance to the next. This gave me a good familiarization with the Ordinances on which I was liable to be consulted at any time by DCs and others. It was also quite an interesting job and Johnny Loveridge seemed pleased with the work I had done. He was always an appreciative man and everyone I knew found it a joy to work for him. He also had a strong sense of humour which he applied to good effect when things seemed to be going wrong as they often did in the latter days of colonial rule. He was never unduly worried by events unless one of his staff was in difficulties somewhere. Then he quickly applied his very agile mind to what should be done. I remember one occasion when my very good friend, Ian Cochran, had some difficulties in the Sefwi District in the far west of the Colony. There were two states, one known as Sefwi Bekwai and the other known as Sefwi Anwiawso. Johnny rang up to find out what was happening and when answered by Ian's chief clerk he was told 'the DC has gone to a riot in Sefwu Bekwai'. Johnny replied 'I thought the trouble was in Sefwi Anwiawso'. 'No, Sir,' came the reply 'that was yesterday's riot'.

After completion of my initial tasks regarding the Krachi District I started on travelling around native courts and inspecting their records and general operations. Colin Russell had worked out a routine for this, but it was always difficult to find out from the records how a court was really working. The courts were heavily dependent upon their registrars, who functioned rather like clerks to lay magistrates in Britain. Unlike clerks to the justices they were far from being trained lawyers and they often had an illiterate panel of members to advise. During his time as Judicial Adviser, Johnny Loveridge had set up an examination for registrars with the aim of establishing certain elementary standards. Later I devised some two day courses for registrars in different parts of the country; these were once again elementary in nature, but at least they gave the registrars a chance to air their problems. Another important task was getting court panels reformed so that more literate persons became court members. Whatever one did it was always necessary to remember that in the Gold Coast there were 'customary gifts' which we regarded as bribes.

Towards the end of 1950 there was much work necessary on the elections to be held early in 1951. For polling day all normal work was set aside and I made my services available to Jack Crawford, the DC of Cape Coast. Jack assigned me to a polling station at a place on the Central Province railway where there had been some problems over registration and complaints about the registration officers, who did not seem to have put many people on the register. Jack told me in his colourful way that everyone coming to the polls would be armed with a Dane gun or a cutlass. I did not take this seriously of course, but there was some complaining and shouting about the allegedly wicked registration officers. When the poll was completed and I was about to leave with the ballot boxes the last words of the villagers about the registration officers were 'And we gave them a bottle of whisky too'. Something had gone wrong over the customary gift.

The elections outside towns such as Cape Coast were conducted on the basis of an electoral college to which successful candidates went to elect a member of the Assembly. I went to help Bill Peters in one of these being held in Elmina. He did not really need any help although at the time he had not been in the Gold Coast for very long. As the wheels of fortune turned he was in fact at the beginning of a distinguished career in the service of the Crown. After leaving the Colonial Service a few years later as most of us had to do he managed to surmount the barriers against getting into the Commonwealth Relations Office. There was opposition to us as ex-colonials getting into the Commonwealth Relations Office, as we were said to be tarred with the colonial brush; this was an argument designed of course to keep out competition. Bill surmounted all this and finished his overseas career first as Ambassador in Uruguay and then as High Commissioner in Malawi.

The elections resulted in an outstanding success for Kwame Nkrumah's CPP. The outcome in urban areas where there were direct elections was not a surprise, but a more balanced result was expected from the rural areas where voting was through electoral colleges. The Governor had an immediate problem in that Kwame Nkrumah had been elected with a large majority whilst still serving a prison sentence in an Accra gaol. Releasing him was inevitable, but Sir Charles had to exercise considerable negotiating skill thereafter; somehow he had to get Nkrumah's cooperation in working the constitution. Fortunately, it became the beginning of a period of cooperation between these two men; both had constituencies to consider. Nkrumah had to consider his followers who had been told that the constitution was bogus and fraudulent and Arden-Clarke had to consider his masters in Whitehall and his own civil service. The latter were perhaps in a sense a tame constituency, but getting willing cooperation was by no means certain and in this Arden-Clarke's skill in communicating and obtaining understanding was very important. Apart from other considerations he made it quite plain that he was going to continue in charge of the service and be responsible for it. Both Arden-Clarke and Nkrumah understood the problems facing the other person and worked together on that basis, although by no means always in agreement. Nkrumah had ambitions as a future pan-African leader beyond his abilities or, indeed, those of any individual, and he was prepared to adopt a tactical approach.

After the elections early in 1951 most things in the country continued with little apparent change. In Accra the Secretariat was reorganized into Ministries with African Ministers drawn from the elected Assembly. Local Government came under Asafu Adjaye, who was a Regional Representative from Ashanti as opposed to a CPP member. He was a highly respected lawyer and by no means filled with revolutionary ideas. In Cape Coast Johnny Loveridge continued in command without change, except for an occasional argument with Meredith Hyde-Clarke, who was Asafu Adjaye's Permanent Secretary. Hyde-Clarke was necessarily suspect anywhere in West Africa, as he had come from East Africa – known as one of the 'wise men from the East'.

For my part I was enjoying the independent nature of my job concerned with Native Courts and trying to help DCs, who became increasingly concerned with the legalities of their jobs; there could no longer be an easy going approach to their powers,

Bungalow no.1

as the local press and CPP members were watchful for any excess of authority. With friends and colleagues in the Chief Commissioner's office like Alan Cowley and Reg Wallace life was never dull. Alan was concerned with Native Authority budgets and accounts whilst Reg was Secretary to the Chief Commissioner. Like most members of the Administration we realised that the days of running the affairs of the country largely by means of a persuasive approach were over. Our role was inevitably changing, probably for the worse, but in the meantime we made the best of things and went happily about our work and social life. The latter was largely of our own making and I particularly remember late snacks after a few bottles of Accra brewed Club Beer in Alan Cowley's house. The routine was for Salifu to be called and asked to provide 'Hammy, cheesy, eggy topside'; as the name might suggest this meant a base of ham with cheese on top and an egg at the summit of the nutritious pile. We all went different ways a few years later. Alan continued for a short time into self-government and then became an estate agent in his native Isle of Man. Sadly he died at a young age. Reg continued in the service in Somaliland, but later took the Home Civil Service examination and got into the Treasury. From there he became Financial Secretary in the Solomon Islands then governed by Sir Michael

Gass also from the Gold Coast. Later Reg became governor of Kiribati in its final phase before independence. Subsequently, he became Financial Secretary in Gibraltar where he has since settled with his third wife, married after being twice widowed. When in Cape Coast like me he was married but temporarily separated as Barbara, like Faith, was looking after a young child in England.

There was some improvement in family matters from my point of view in that Faith was able to join me for a few months in Cape Coast, as my parents looked after Nigel for a short period. It made a welcome break and she found life in Cape Coast more comfortable than it had been a few years earlier. We were living in a house which had been occupied by the DC of Cape Coast for many years and in general housing conditions were being improved. We already had a septic tank toilet and whilst Faith was there the thunder box in the spare quarters was replaced by a septic tank. An amusing incident occurred one morning when the Irish Foreman of Works in charge of the operations arrived and let forth his usual rhetoric of barrack room language to exhort the labourers, not knowing that Faith was sitting at the breakfast table. He marched into the house as he had done when I was on my own and then apologetically and sheepishly retreated. The poor man had found there was a woman in the house.

A view of Kumasi
Canham Collection
published by kind
permission of
Cambridge
University Library

Unfortunately, Faith had to return to England before I went to Ashanti as JA there. The theoretical plan was that there should be a Senior JA and one JA in Cape Coast and one JA in Kumasi in charge of the Ashanti Native Courts. In practice there was rarely more than one in each place. Colin Russell disappeared into the newly formed Ministries in Accra leaving John Matson as Senior JA and myself as the junior. With the incidence of leave and various other events John and I quite frequently found ourselves doing the job both at Cape Coast and Kumasi. It was fairly typical of the way in which staffing in practice differed greatly from the theory.

An Ashanti Chief
with his Entourage
Canham Collection
published by kind
permission of
Cambridge
University Library

I found the move to Ashanti very interesting. The Ashantis were a proud people grouped around an Asantehene, Prempeh II. In earlier history when the British were becoming established as the ascendent European nation in the Gold Coast there had

been much conflict. The British found the Ashantis a nuisance, as they frequently raided the Fanti people of the coast to take slaves. Early in the nineteenth century George Maclean as head of the British merchants who held the reins of power operating from Cape Coast made peace with the Ashantis. He functioned rather like a District Commissioner in later times with few powers but an ability to negotiate. Unfortunately, others who came later as Governors after the country came under the Crown functioned in a more militant manner. There were a number of expeditions against Ashanti and Sir Garnet Wolseley sacked Kumasi in 1874 before withdrawing, but this did not solve the problem. In 1900 Governor Hodgson led another expedition and really upset the Ashantis by demanding the Golden Stool, which was of course hidden. Prempeh I was later deported to the Seychelles from where he was not allowed to return until 1924. Ashanti was annexed to the British Crown in 1901 and was thereafter administered by a Chief Commissioner under the Governor. Recognition of the Ashanti Confederacy was granted during the governorship of Sir Shenton Thomas (1932–34).

When I went to Kumasi in 1951 to take up the post of Judicial Adviser Prempeh II was Asantehene and Hugh Beeton was Chief Commissioner. I had worked under Hugh Beeton in Tarkwa and I enjoyed working for him once again. He was not as colourful a character as Johnny Loveridge in Cape Coast, but he possessed a great ability to get his staff all working in the same direction. The Ashanti Administration, like the Ashanti people, had a pride in belonging to it; this sometimes caused resentment when persons transferred to the Colony tactlessly talked about how things worked better in Ashanti. Generally the administration in Ashanti worked more smoothly, as it should have done with a smaller area centred on Kumasi. The communications all ran towards Kumasi and it was fairly easy for the Chief Commissioner to arrange monthly meetings with his DCs. In the Colony arranging such a meeting at much less frequent intervals required more organization.

The monthly meetings with Hugh Beeton in the Chair gave everyone the chance to discuss problems of mutual interest and enabled Hugh to communicate various things in an informal manner. The meetings were conducted in a convivial atmosphere and I was called upon for legal advice from time to time. My old friend Arthur Davies, who was DC of Kumasi, brought up an interesting question at the end of a meeting. 'Can you tell us about knocking fees?' The term tended to raise a laugh; it was originally applied to payment by a prospective bridegroom to the lady's father on announcing his intentions. The fee originally took the form of a gift in kind, such as a sheep, and was payable on knocking on the door of the prospective bride's father. The payment of the fees became applied to the seeking of any favour and when this spilt over into public life it naturally was disapproved by expatriate government officials. Corruption was something that we regarded as at the root of much evil, but Arthur in fact had a very good point in that we often failed to appreciate where customary gifts ended and corruption began. It was, indeed, almost impossible to draw a line. Arthur pursued his legal interests by reading for the Bar after his retirement; thereafter he spent some years in charge of the Oxford University Lodgings Delagacy, which was concerned with licensed lodgings for undergraduates. We had both been at Magdalen College together and I was happy on several occasions to renew my acquaintance with the college in his company. Arthur also served as DC in Sunyani in the North West of Ashanti. Whilst there he had a nasty experience with a rabid dog. Jean and his family were in contact with this dog, whilst he avoided it by jumping on the desk in his office, but they were all advised after an autopsy of the dog's brain in Accra to have the anti-rabies injections. At that time these consisted of injections in the stomach and were not very pleasant. Arthur's sense of humour did not, however, desert him when he told the story of how the telegram sent back from Accra after the autopsy read 'Dog rabid and should be destroyed immediately'. Compliance with this instruction was a little difficult when the head was already in Accra. Arthur was a man of considerable administrative ability and charm, who sadly died at a relatively young age.

An interesting job which came in my direction whilst I was in Ashanti was hearing a land case in the Northern Territories. Unlike the rest of the country in which DCs were not allowed to hear land cases, in the Northern Territories it was part of their judicial duties. In this particular case, however, practically every DC in the NTs had at some time been concerned with trying to settle the case administratively and so could not function judicially. Geoffrey Burden, the Chief Commissioner of the Northern Territories, wanted the case settled and had the idea of getting me gazetted as a DC in the NTs and assigned to hear the case. Hugh Beeton agreed to release me for this task and so I found myself in Bolagatanga in February, 1952, just after the death of King George VI. The case was between the Na Yeri, Chief of Mamprussi, one of the large states of the NTs and the Sandemanab, a much smaller chief. The David and Goliath comparison is hardly apt in that the Sandemanab was a large tall man whilst the Na Yeri, the much more important chief, was a relatively small man.

Peter Helps, the DC of Bolagatanga, was naturally concerned about security whilst the case was being heard as some twenty or thirty lorry loads of supporters from the two sides were expected to come into Bolagatanga. I was quite confident that he had the situation under control, but two lawyers from Accra engaged on opposite sides were not so happy; they had not been to the NTs before and were perhaps naturally a little alarmed. Bossman and Ollenu were quite well known to me and came to see me in the rest house before the case started. They sought time to file pleadings and suggested that I should adjourn the case in the hope that at a later date the situation would have calmed down. I could not see any reason why it should and said I thought we should go ahead with the case; I was of course mindful of all the organization that had gone into getting everything arranged for the hearing. I could also imagine Geoffrey Burden's reaction if I returned to Kumasi with the case unheard. When the lawyers had left I rushed to my law books, as I was not quite certain whether the two lawyers could demand the right to pleadings. I was happy to find the matter was discretionary and when in court ruled that we should have a brief statement from each side instead of formal pleadings.

The security arrangements were in the hands of the Native Authority Police who differed greatly from their counterparts further south. The courthouse was open at the sides below a grass roof with low walls from which the public could watch when there was no more room in court. Any doubts about the competence of the police that I might have had would have been quickly removed when I asked to be allowed a gap in the solid wall of humanity at the side to allow a little air into the building; a word from the police sergeant produced a rapid dispersal.

The case was interesting in that the Sandemaneb was claiming that his lands extended up to the White Volta and included three villages on his side of the river. The evidence from the villages was largely contrary to that claim, but it was clear that they had originally been on the river bank. Some years earlier the people had migrated from the bank when it was found that river blindness caused by the simulum fly was largely confined to the river area. I made a visit there whilst the case was adjourned over a week-end and found the area by the river almost deserted.

The river would have been a convenient boundary and there are many instances all over the world of rivers being used in that way although they often form a link between people on opposite banks. In this instance I found for the Na Yeri against the claim to the river boundary line. I was happy a year or two later to hear that my decision was upheld by the West African Court of Appeal (WACA said as one word as it was known). The Sandemaneb said he was going to the Privy Council on further appeal which was possible from Colonies, but the case did not go any further. One of the main grounds for appeal was that the Commissioner (it was I) had not gone into the case with sufficient diligence, but WACA found on the contrary that it had been heard with very great care. I was very fortunate in having Bossman and Ollenu as counsel in the case; they not only put their clients' cases very ably but as befits good barristers they were very helpful to the court.

I found Kumasi a very friendly place and I was able both to pursue old friendships and form some new ones. A person I had known elsewhere with whom I spent some time in the evenings was the District Magistrate, Willy Van Lare. He had been called to Bar in England and returned to practise as a barrister in Accra for some time before being appointed to the Judiciary. He told me a story of his early experiences when he had to raise his fees at the request of his clients in Togoland. When he told them his fee in a land case they insisted that he should double it as they knew the other side would be paying more for their counsel. African barristers were often thought to overcharge their clients, but here was a case where the clients thought otherwise and did not like it. Willy later became a judge and was appointed to the Ghana Court of Appeal after Independence. He and his two brother judges were dismissed summarily from office when they quashed the convictions of two opponents of Kwami Nkrumah. After Nkrumah was overthrown by a military government Willy became High Commissioner in Canada, but sadly suffered an illness from which he died.

Another friend in Kumasi was my next door neighbour Judge Quashie-Idun. One evening I received my first and last apology from a judge when he came around following an argument between members of our respective staff. I had been growing some lettuces and Paul, my cook, was incensed to find the judge's young turkeys being reared by his wife had come through the fence and eaten them all. I did not enter into any discussion on the law relating to trespassing turkeys; there was the further point that they were young turkeys – comparable perhaps with child trespassers.

At various times whilst I was in Kumasi in the Chief Commissioner's Office there were Brian Smith, John Dixon, Bob Kingston and Charles Carrington. I had known or worked with them all somewhere else at different times and the latter two were particular rivals on the golf course. I could give a good game to Bob, but Charles was far too steady for my erratic play. I continued playing with Charles for many years after the Gold Coast days with much enjoyment although similar lack

A station on the railway line to Kumasi
Canham Collection published by kind permission of Cambridge University Library

of success. One of Charles' attributes was his rendering of almost any part of the Gilbert and Sullivan operas, and I also regarded them as having appropriate humour for West African life. I only found Charles depressed on one occasion when he was in hospital with hepatitis. This is of course a depressing illness and it was quite common in West Africa. Happily, depression was not something from which my colleagues in the Gold Coast seemed to suffer. There could have been plenty of reason for it, but it rarely happened and stress, another modern illness, was something expected of life to be taken in one's stride. We probably all had it, but preferred not to talk about it, or called it 'fever' – the term normally used for malaria.

If ever I needed to dispel gloom a visit to Donald and Carol Hardy in Sunyani was a sure way of doing so. Donald had been a member of the Indian Civil Service and Carol had been brought up in India, being the daughter of an American missionary family. Both adapted without apparent difficulty to the Gold Coast and their second son was born whilst I was in Kumasi. Donald believed in the efficient ways he had learnt in the ICS before Indian independence, but he was prepared to temper them. This was sometimes necessary and I particularly remember a visit we made together to Dorma. He went through the Native Authority accounts whilst I looked at the court record books; both left much to be desired. The staff there were fairly competent people, but I think they had tended to regard themselves as a remoter area in the west of Ashanti to which normal rules need not apply.

Donald Hardy's district also extended to Wenchi, which was now a sub-district under Donald as Senior DC. At one stage Gordon Edwards was in charge of this sub-district. He was a colourful character and unlike most of us in the service he had some inherited wealth. He was not an ostentatious man but he liked to keep a good house and regarded himself as father of his people in the vein of DCs of a much earlier time, who had a more baronial approach to their offices. He thought a Rolls Royce would be the ideal vehicle for the Gold Coast roads and he acquired a slightly smaller model of Rolls produced soon after World War II. This was not, however, ideal for roads requiring a large ground clearance height and he then decided to get a Land Rover. He applied for a loan from Government to buy this which caused Hugh Beeton some serious thought over whether the owner of a Rolls should be granted an interest free loan by Government. He obtained his loan and kept his Rolls for town running, but there was not much town in Wenchi. One of Gordon's charming eccentricities was putting warning notices where road labourers were at work reading 'Gentlemen at work', and if anyone thought this unusual he insisted 'they are gentlemen'. There was a history of civil unrest in Wenchi largely surrounding the Wenchihene (Chief of Wenchi). On one occasion when there was a riot around the Ahinfie (Chief's house) Gordon decided to put on his ceremonial uniform and go there on a horse. The rioters were so surprised by this spectacle that they dispersed without more ado.

Gordon Edwards also featured in the local press when the Governor decided that it was time to abandon the ageing Government House Humber and get a more dignified Rolls. The Government House drivers were sent to Wenchi for training on Gordon's smaller Rolls, which the press described as the DC's mini-Rolls; Gordon was both amused and incensed by this term. He was one of the Administration who really enjoyed being a DC and found himself a niche for a time after Independence in the Northern Territories, but eventually he retired to his native Merioneth. Unlike most of us he was not troubled by having to find something to make ends meet, but by all accounts he was not particularly happy until his death at a relatively early age. It was a privilege to have been one of his friends.

Another trek I undertook with Donald Hardy took us to the rest house in the west of the district allegedly haunted by the ghost of a DC who died there. There was a story that steward boys laid two places at table whenever anyone alone stayed there so that provision was made for the ghost. As Donald and I were together we wondered whether there would be a third place, but this did not happen and there were no nocturnal noises apart from that of the rodent population in the roof. Could the ghost have been rats?

Our travels on this occasion also took us across the French Ivory Coast border to visit the Commandant (DC) of Bondoukou. He apologised to us for the state of his house since his wife had returned to France. We could not see anything wrong with it, but then the French mesdames tended to keep servants on their toes, rather than adopt the more British indirect rule approach. The latter worked much better if the lady of the house had to leave it from time to time whilst they attended to the needs of children in Britain or elsewhere. The latter method was also much more educative for the staff, and in the case of my own household Faith could rightly claim that it enabled Atta, the 'small boy' to move up rapidly after we left to become cook and steward for a bishop.

The Commandant took Donald and me to see the airstrip he had built near Bondoukou. He was proud of this as it formed part of the French strategy for dealing with possible unrest in enabling them to move gendarmes or troops rapidly to any trouble spot. When we asked the commandant how he would deal with any trouble he replied with the one word *mitrailieuse* (machine gun). There was, however, a more human side to his life in Africa as we found on returning to the town when two attractive looking girls waved to him from the roadside; after waving back at them holding the steering wheel rather precariously in one hand his simple words were *'Amies du Commandant'*.

My service in Ashanti was divided by some eight months in the UK in 1952. In the latter days of the Colonial Service there was a recognition of the need for more training for Administrative Officers. A circular set out the plans for an inaugural course similar to the course I took in 1939 followed by another course about five or six years later. There was a short paragraph at the end saying that officers of my seniority who had missed the second course could apply for other forms of training. I applied to spend six months in a barrister's chambers part of the time being taken out of my leave. To my great surprise this was approved, leaving the arrangements to be made by me. The result was that I spent three months in criminal law chambers and three months in chambers mainly concerned with civil law. In the first case I was a pupil of James Burge. He later became a QC and was engaged on the defence of Stephen Ward, who was charged with spying offences connected with the Profumo affair. James Burge was an able cross-examiner, who made the charges against his client seem completely outrageous. He met his match, however, in Mandy Rice-Davies who alleged as a prosecution witness that certain improprieties had taken place between her and another person concerned in the affair. James Burge put the point to her that the person with whom these amorous incidents were alleged to have taken place would deny that anything of the kind happened. Her quick reply has passed into linguistic history in a number of forms. Her words were reported to be 'He would say that, wouldn't he?' My later three months with Leonard Halpern were a more relaxed affair, but in some ways more instructive. There was time for discussion whereas in the criminal law chambers there tended to be a rush between the Old Bailey, the Middlesex Sessions, Bow Street and elsewhere.

The time spent in England in 1952 was very busy, as Faith and I acquired the house in which we still live and settled Nigel at a boarding school. We paid £3000 for the house, but we have extended it much more expensively on a number of occasions. The house was unremarkable and fairly sound in essentials, having been built in 1947, but it was on an acre of uncultivated land with an orchard, old pigsties and other old buildings. The previous owner had a taxi service and repaired old farm machinery in his spare time. Unfortunately, much of the machinery must have been unrepairable and this was dumped around the site. We found a scrap iron merchant who took what he wanted and promised to come back for the rest; this as we might have expected did not happen. We eventually found a dump and took away seven trailer loads; perhaps we should have started a museum. The pigsties must have been occupied fairly recently as one evening a pig came down the drive looking for its way home pursued by its present owner. It was all a very enjoyable time as Faith and I rarely managed to get as long as eight months together.

CHAPTER XIII

Independence Approaches

I RETURNED TO ASHANTI at the end of 1952. I travelled by air on the trans-Saharan route to Accra, which took about nineteen hours from Heathrow; this was still an airport of Nissen huts, but none the less a welcoming place.

There were few visible changes in the way things were run in the Gold Coast, but talks on the future had been going on between the Governor and Kwame Nkrumah, who had been granted the title of Prime Minister; previously he had been Leader of Government Business. It was clear to both Sir Charles Arden-Clarke and Kwame Nkrumah that there had to be rapid moves towards independence and that a suitable constitution had to be developed. Sir Charles knew that the Gold Coast would again become very difficult to govern if there was too much postponement of independence. He had, however, to convince the Colonial Office of this and there was some alarm being expressed to this Office by Sir John Macpherson, the Governor of Nigeria. There was a meeting of the two Governors at the Colonial Office, but it was not practicable to hold back independence for Ghana simply because Nigeria could not move forward at the same pace. The problems in Nigeria were far greater owing to the disparity between the Muslim North with its strong political institutions in the Emirates and the more westernized South with greater economic strength and more political sophistication.

The problems in the Gold Coast were by no means trivial. The reliance of the civil service on expatriate staff in most of its senior posts was a major problem, especially as these members of staff were mostly part of a unified service under the Secretary of State for the Colonies. This was a condition of service which could not in fairness to the staff be abandoned with staff being required to serve an independent government. The situation was unsettling for members of the Colonial Service, but in general there was a confidence arising from past experience that we would be fairly treated. As a result we went about our work with a 'business as usual' attitude and there was very little, if any, loss of morale.

In Ashanti in the early months of 1953 there was not any notable sign of the opposition to the CPP which was to occur later. Nkrumah was still on his political honeymoon. My own work with Native Courts after my return from leave towards the end of 1952 continued much where I had left off. There was, however, one rather unusual incident when I arranged to meet Michael McMullen at a court in a village outside Kumasi and found it in turmoil. Michael had earlier found the panel members unable to emerge from their office following an unpopular decision. By the time I had arrived reasonable order had been restored, but it was still necessary to get the police to ensure that the president of the court and his fellows could remain unmolested. Mike was not particularly disturbed by the incident and remarked 'Now you really know how a native court works'. I met Mike in London from time to time later where he was practising at the Bar and then some years later I learnt he had become a Crown Court judge. Recently I have met him again at old Ashanti gatherings; it is interesting how the rapport amongst people who served in Ashanti still persists.

The Certificating of native court registrars required an annual examination. Setting the papers was quite interesting, but marking them was a tedious chore. I also held short training courses of a few days duration to give some hope to those that failed and to offer an opportunity to others to discuss their problems. It was a much more rewarding occupation than reading through examination papers, but there had to be some means of awarding certificates and thus giving Native Authorities some standard based on which they could employ registrars. On one occasion when I had to mark a registrars' examination I spent two days in the Rest House by Lake Bosumtwi. The Rest House was a fairly isolated one and overlooked the lake; this formed an unusual feature in forest country. The lake was volcanic in its origins and was simply formed by small streams draining into the volcanic crater. The scenery was unique for the Gold Coast, which was lacking in diversity of scenery over many parts of the country.

Whilst the Gold Coast was searching for the way forward to independence there were many visitors from Britain who were expert in their field. One I remember particularly was A. E. Young a former Commissioner of the Metropolitan Police. Amongst other things he was asked to advise on the Native Authority Police and in this context a meeting was held in the Chief Commissioner's Office. A prominent CPP member at this meeting was Krobo Edusei, who contrasted how in London the policemen helped him to find his way around whereas during the troubles in Kumasi an expatriate policeman had beaten him with a baton. As befitted an old hand at all levels of police work former Commissioner Young listened with an absolutely impassive face. I did not doubt that in his mind he could detect the difference between Krobo Edusei as a visitor to London and Krobo Edusei as a rioter in Kumasi. Krobo was a colourful character who at one time became Minister of the Interior. He described his Ministry as a double-edged sword which he intended to wield with both edges. On another occasion he was reported as replying to a somewhat unparliamentary remark in the Assembly by saying – 'I am not a rat; he must not call me a rat; if I am a rat, he is a rat too.' A collection of the works and sayings of Krobo Edusei could have made interesting reading if it had been written.

Increasing interest in the Gold Coast arising from the general situation brought politicians amongst others to see things at first hand. One such visitor was Mrs Eirene White (later Baroness White). One of her particular interests was in Togoland, but she had been advised not to go there, owing to some local political turmoil arising from Togo Union opposition to unity with the Gold Coast. She came to Kumasi instead, and I was invited, amongst others, by Hugh and Mary Beeton to meet her at the Residency (Chief Commissioner's house). I was engaged upon a quiet conversation with her over coffee after dinner and mentioned Togoland. Thereafter she became somewhat emotional in her expressing sympathy for the Ewes as unhappy divided people between British and French territories. I agreed that the original settlement had been inconsiderate, but I said it was not oppressive now and many Ewes made quite a good thing out of it. I stupidly went on to say that there was some political nonsense arising from it whereupon she exclaimed so that everyone in the room could hear – 'What do you mean by political nonsense?' Happily Mary Beeton calmed the situation with an offer of more coffee.

Visitors who came to the Gold Coast to advise on various subjects included an O&M (Organization and Methods) man, who was loaned to the Government for a fee by Urwick Orr and Company. He was in Kumasi for some time, where he spent his evenings with different members of Government Departments. I had his company for one such evening. I thought he was going around to gather information and opinions, but I was treated to a lengthy dissertation on how he organized a Northampton boot factory; I could not quite see how the boot factory was going to help us. Our problem was more to do with organizing the increasing amount of paper that seemed to arise from political and administrative changes.

I was fortunate in Kumasi in having Mr Wemegah as a clerk in my office to look after the paper which came into it. He tended to be very slow which sometimes exasperated me unreasonably, but he had two great attributes – a very good memory for anything he had seen and a delightfully cheerful nature. He needed the latter to get over a very frustrating personal matter. He kept taking the examination for executive officers only to find it cancelled several times because the papers were found to have been 'leaked' beforehand – rather like Government documents in Britain now. His legal knowledge was not great, but he excelled himself later when Johnny Loveridge was Chief Commissioner in Ashanti over an application for a special licence for a marriage. He went into the Chief Commissioner's office with a special licence ready for signature. On being asked why this should be granted he said – 'When you see the lady, Sir, you will agree it is a case of res ipsa loquitur'. Johnny saw the lady, signed the licence and was glad she left the office without the need to send for a midwife. The legal doctrine of 'res ipsa loquitur' was one established during the nineteenth century in the development of the law of negligence and generally referred to cases such as a bag of flour falling out of a shop onto somebody's head. It really meant that the thing spoke for itself and required no further proof, so it was quite a good analogy, although an unusual use of the terminology.

I was very glad it was possible for Faith to join me in Kumasi at the beginning of May, 1953, but it was only a short time

Faith with her
Holy Child School
class

before we moved to Cape Coast, where I took over the job of acting Senior Judicial Adviser; I filled this post for most of the remaining two and a half years of my time in the Gold Coast. There was a system of acting allowances which was very welcome as our finances were not very flush after buying our house in England and sending Nigel to a boarding school. John Matson was the substantive Senior Judicial Adviser, but he was nearly always filling a different post in an acting capacity. The move to Cape Coast was very welcome to Faith as she was able to resume teaching at the Holy Child College and we had a pleasant house there with some sea breezes.

I enjoyed working with Johnny Loveridge again as my Chief Commissioner, although it was only for a limited period, as towards the end of the year the Colony Administration was split up into three regions and Johnny went to become the CCNT (Chief Commissioner Northern Territories). One of the first tasks given to me by Johnny Loveridge on arrival in Cape Coast was enquiring into a very tragic event. Whilst I was still in Ashanti Edgar Brooks, whom I knew well, had been murdered in an incident outside Elmina Castle. There were long-standing feuds between the people of Elmina town and those of the surrounding villages. These quarrels went back as far as the days of the Dutch in Elmina Castle, whose local relationships were not very good. In the present instance the contention was in the main over rates being collected in the villages and the money going into Elmina – something that was frequently unpopular in rural areas.

Arising from the non-payment of rates two Native Authority policemen had been sent to a neighbouring village to make an arrest. As frequently happened in such cases they were chased out of the village; in local parlance this was often referred to as 'taking to their heels'. Unfortunately on leaving they took a drum with them, which greatly incensed the villagers as drums had symbolic significance. The Gold Coast police were aware that there was trouble in the area, but the facts about the drum were probably not known and the DC of Cape Coast was not kept informed about the affair. The incident connected with the drum led to a night of stirring up indignation in the villages around Elmina and much drinking took place. In the morning large crowds with shotguns being carried started moving down the road to Elmina.

Edgar Brooks was in charge of the Police Mobile Unit housed in Elmina Castle. The Unit was held available for disorder anywhere in the western part of the Colony and it was very unwise of local people to move into Elmina with the intent of recovering their drum when this force lay just across the bridge leading into the town. Edgar knew there was some frequent trouble between the Elmina people and those outside, but he probably did not know about the incident concerning the drum, or how serious the trouble could become. When early in the morning he saw from his quarters in the castle that a mob was advancing down the road, he quickly collected about a dozen men and put a cordon across the road. They were armed only with their batons, although there were a number of shotguns being carried by members of the mob. One person amongst them shouted 'Shoot the white man'. Sadly that was exactly what someone with a shotgun did and Edgar Brooks was killed instantly. The man who fired the shot was felled by a policeman with a baton and killed, but it was never established who instigated the shooting; he may have died too. An armed party came out of the castle and some shots were fired. Thereafter the mob fled and some thirty people were killed caused by both police firing and the general stampede taking its toll. The villages from which the mob came were deserted by all except a few goats, even two weeks later; such was the fear engendered by the police action after the shooting. The police were undoubtedly incensed, but proper discipline was soon restored when John Coles, a former Palestinian policeman, arrived to take charge.

I was asked to put together a factual report, so that Johnny Loveridge could resist any pressure from Accra for a public enquiry. He thought, rightly in my opinion, that any such enquiry would lead to recriminations and do more harm than good. I was glad later that there was no suggestion of a public enquiry and the tragic incident was left closed apart from Police investigations.

The shout from someone in the mob about shooting the white man was probably not part of any racially motivated feeling but rather an identification of the person in charge of the opposition to the riotous objective of the mob. There was remarkably little anti-white feeling amongst ordinary people, although politicians were trying to build it up; their general political approach was that white rulers were holding back progress and without white people around everyone would be better off in every way. Animosity towards individuals ran contrary to natural Ghanaian friendliness and good manners, so I never felt any hostility to me personally. Some people did not like what I did or what I represented, but I am sure most of my colleagues would agree that this led to very little personal unfriendliness.

There was an amusing incident observed by Faith shortly after our arrival back in Cape Coast. I had left her in the car whilst going to pay for some petrol and someone shouted 'White man go home'. Someone else seeing Faith said 'Not you madam, white woman stay'. Then someone else added 'she be teacher'. Perhaps the message was that DCs are bad for us, but we want teachers. The conclusion might be that our only justification for being in Africa was as teachers. However, that would be an oversimplification since our educative function required a background of law and order. Then there was the need for law and order also so that commerce could flourish without which there could be no generation of the wealth needed for education. These are purely academic questions, but from a social point of view there was very little, if any, antipathy in the Gold Coast between white and black people. A large amount of credit for this must be given to Ghanaians for their friendliness and tolerance. I should be happy if I could feel that in turn they are accepted with equal friendliness in Britain.

A more interesting and less distressing job given to me by Johnny Loveridge was enquiring into the conditions for employees on timber concessions. The timber industry had developed substantially after the end of World War II with the need for hardwoods in European countries and elsewhere. The granting of concessions to timber companies had resulted in the setting up of small labour camps. Whereas in the mining industry these were governed by Mining Health Areas legislation there was nothing comparable for the timber industry. I was assisted in the task by a Forestry Officer and a member of the Medical Department. We were pleasantly surprised to find that on the whole conditions for the labour force on Timber Concessions were satisfactory, but we recommended that there should be some regulations for health and welfare. Johnny Loveridge was glad to learn that there was nothing particularly worrying; he was always trying to keep ahead of potential problems. The general policy of the Forestry Department regarding timber concessions was to allow concessions fairly freely outside Forest Reserves within which felling was strictly controlled. It would have been beyond the resources of the Department to do more outside concessions beyond encouraging systems of felling which gave scope for natural regeneration.

Soon after Faith and I arrived in Cape Coast we made a short return visit to Kumasi for the Coronation celebrations in June, 1953, and attended a very impressive parade staged by the Gold Coast Regiment in the presence of the Asantehene and his subordinate Chiefs. On the way to Kumasi we met a tropical storm just north of Bekwai. A large tree was brought down across the road blocking our way. Fortunately we were able to turn round and go back to Bekwai, where Mike Patteson, the DC, looked after us until the road was reported to have been cleared. This was achieved by cross-cut saws operated by two men with remarkable speed considering the size of the large rain forest tree. We also attended some less elaborate celebrations in Cape Coast where we spent the actual day of the Coronation listening to redifussion radio.

Most of my travelling connected with Native Courts was to the eastern part of the country where there seemed to be more problems. Difficulties of a political nature arose over the Akim

Abuakwa Native Court. The headquarters of the old Native Authority in Kibi had been dominated by the Ofori Atta family with which Danquah had connections. He was now opposed to Nkrumah and the CPP; this party now dominated the Native Authority and removed the headquarters outside Kibi. This problem also affected the Native Court, which contrary to the wishes of the Native Authority continued to sit in Kibi. I tried to explain that it could sit in two divisions and should in any event sit where it was convenient to the public. It was all to no avail. On my return to Cape Coast I had to give an account of my failure to Johnny Loveridge, who was most understanding of the problems I had met. Johnny took everything in his stride and was not perturbed by little local difficulties. He sensed that I was feeling a little tense in having to tell him of my failure and broke off the conversation to draw attention to two lizards cavorting on his verandah. When I had finished he said perhaps getting agreement will be the biggest thing after Panmunjon. At the time the agreement at Panmunjon had just brought the Korean War to an end. Unfortunately, I achieved no such agreement and the Akim Abuakwa court caused me much trouble later. However, the incident in 1953 was one of many things that made me regard Johnny Loveridge as the best boss I ever had. He knew how to get me and many others to give their best work; he did not add to pressures that were already there, but helped and encouraged. Before he left Cape Coast later in 1953 we had a number of golf matches on the Cape Coast course with Stewart Lawson and Ian Cochran, as the two real golfers taking part. Johnny like me was inclined to land his ball in the bush from time to time. The last match was played over 18 holes instead of the usual nine. At the 17th hole Ian and I both had our balls near the green (they were actually browns being sand constructed) when Johnny shouted to Stewart from the bush 'can I do any good?'. On being told that he could he made a remarkable shot putting his ball a few feet from the hole and won it. This made us all square with one to play, but we decided to call it an honourable draw as we could not see to play another hole. Darkness descended quite quickly after sunset in the Gold Coast.

When I went on my travels Faith often had to stay behind as she was teaching at the Holy Child College. Whilst I was away she often spent more time on domestic matters in our different residences which in Cape Coast alternated between bungalows Number 1 and Number 6. On one occasion in 1953 when we were occupying the former she was horrified to find that Atta's wife did not have a bed other than the floor for her baby. Faith looked in the garage for something better and her eyes fell upon my old tin bath. These items were sold to young cadets by tropical outfitters and were designed to be used also as packages with a lid fixed with a strap. Mine had travelled from place to place without being unpacked for some time; its contents were unknown, but Paul thought he remembered some old cushions being inside. When opened some movement was observed and a python raised its head causing considerable alarm to all except the garden boy Umaru Moshi. Faith and the others retreated whilst Umaru killed the unfortunate python which had to vacate its living quarters in favour of Atta's baby. When I returned I told Faith that a python was not a particularly dangerous snake, not having a poisonous bite, although its habits were not all pleasant. It gets its food by wrapping itself round its prey, which it squeezes to death.

At times it seemed that the Administrative Service was being slowly squeezed to death. Towards the end of 1953 the Colony was divided like Caesar's Gaul into three parts. This was not an exact return to the three provinces of the days before a Chief Commissioner for the Colony was established; the three divisions were a Western Region covering in effect the old Western and Central Provinces, an Eastern Region covering most of the old Eastern Province and a Trans-Volta Region covering the areas east of Volta River including the Trusteeship Territory of Togoland. Amongst colleagues in Cape Coast there was an inevitable feeling that the policy was one designed to divide and rule from Accra. On the other hand it is doubtful whether an administrative officer of less ability than Johnny Loveridge could have run the area with the increasing complexity of dealing with different ministries in Accra. Johnny Loveridge succeeded Geoffrey Burden in the Northern Territories and he maintained his existing rank although re-named Chief Regional Officer. The Chief Commissioner of Ashanti was similarly titled, but in the Colony the administrative heads were titled as Regional Officers.

Brian Smith took over as Regional Officer of the Western Region and was a little unwise in extolling the way in which things worked in Ashanti. This led Stewart Lawson to write a little doggerel verse to amuse us all. In a manner customary in the Colonial Service this made the new broom more acceptable. I knew Brian and his enthusiasms well and he soon realized things were not quite so easy. Ashanti was an old established African State with a recognized head situated in Kumasi in the middle of the Region from which

the Chief Regional Officer administered the area as Chief
Commissioners had done for many years. My job changed little,
except that I had to deal with three regions instead of one as well
as Ashanti. I was also required by Brian to locate myself in the
Assistant Chief Commissioner's office for a month and act as his
right-hand man, whilst the post awaited Michael Gass. I managed to accommodate all these jobs with an earlier start at 7.00
a.m. and a shorter lunch break. This led Faith to ask me when
Michael Gass arrived whether he had come to do what I did
between 7.0 a. m. and 8.00 a.m. I had to explain that it was not
quite like that and many Judicial Adviser jobs awaited me when
I returned to the calm of my own office next to the library.

As well as her teaching Faith was becoming concerned in
another matter which occasionally caused her some inconven-
ience in the morning. It was all admirably summed up by Atta,
who remarked upon her lack of interest in breakfast with the
words 'Madam no eat, madam vomit; I think she catch piccin'.
There is hardly a neater term for pregnancy than 'catching
piccin'. Faith had been thinking there was not much doubt
about the matter, so Atta confirmed her diagnosis. There had
probably been a committee discussing the matter amongst the
staff, but it took Atta's forthrightness to resolve the question.

Shortly before Christmas Faith had to go home for Nigel's
Christmas holidays. Fortunately, she was feeling well at this
stage as she had to cope with opening up our house again and
preparing for Christmas. I was left on my own but happily we
had many friends in Cape Coast. On Christmas Day the Brian
Smiths held a party in the evening. In the morning Brian had
telephoned to ask if I would like to go up to Government
Lodge (as the former Chief Commissioner's house was still
known) for a game of snooker. He said he would be on his
own as Margaret and Angela (his daughter) were going to
church. He said he was not going as he reckoned he had served
his time at church when as a son of a parsonage he had to go
at least twice every Sunday and also on saints' days.

The thing I remember particularly about the evening party
was an incident on the journey home. My house was approached
by a sharply rising drive off the main road. Just over the brow
of the hill there was a dark patch, which I approached with

caution, as there appeared to be a palm frond or something in the road. To my surprise the shadow slowly moved and stood up. On driving up alongside I found that I had come upon a sleeping policeman. His words were 'Sorry Sir, my belly spoil'. His Christmas celebrations had obviously got the better of him on his night patrol work, so I simply explained to him that he had not chosen a very good place to try to recover. I have often wondered how credible my story would have sounded if on my way home from a Christmas party I had run over a sleeping policeman. I do not suppose there are many people who have ever seen a real live sleeping policeman in the road.

Between Christmas and the New Year I made a visit to Kibi to try to do something towards resolving the dispute between the two political factions on the panel of the Akim Abuakwa court. This was an almost impossible task, but I spent a very pleasant few days with Dennis Earle going around the district. The evening before I returned to Cape Coast seemed unusually cool on his verandah. I realized later that the Harmattan had set in and that I had become chilled. On my way back to Cape Coast I began to feel unwell and it did not take me long to know that I was suffering from malaria. It was quite commonly brought on by a chill or some other stress to the system; when living in West Africa the parasites were usually lurking some-where, particularly in the spleen. I was not ill for more than a day or two, but I had one night when I could not sleep. At about 4.00 a.m. Atta decided it was the day for polishing the floor and in order to dry off his thick layer of wax polish he put the fan on at full power. This resounded upstairs and put an end to the night for me. The next night was New Year's Eve and I slept soundly into 1954. On New Year's Day I was unable to drink my customary beer at lunchtime but I was persuaded that a glass of pink gin with plenty of bitters would be good for me; it did no harm. The news of my indisposition and unusual gin drinking spread around the land and for several weeks when I spoke to colleagues on the telephone I had to convince them that I was well again.

One of my interesting tasks was holding local authority enquiries. These were held when there was any problem over the Local Authority to succeed the Native Authority under the reorganization of local government. In the Northern Territories there had to be an enquiry in the case of Mamprussi. Whilst travelling there, unbeknown to me beforehand, I had to pass through an area which had been declared smallpox infected. The Medical Department very efficiently set up road blocks at all entrances manned by vaccinators who had to vaccinate anyone and everyone who could not produce a certificate. I had left my certificate at home, so I had to submit to a roadside vaccination. A thing which worried me slightly was the procedure by which the vaccinating implement was very carefully sterilized in a flame but then put down on a dirty-looking cloth before being used to vaccinate me. I pointed this out, but it was thought trivial; I was very happy when the vaccination showed no signs of taking.

The enquiry into Mamprussi was not particularly interesting as there were few grounds for any change from the existing boundaries of the Native Authority which seemed to work very well. However, I found the visit to the North and staying in some of the long established rest houses very interesting. There were record books going back to the beginning of the century and senior visitors clearly paid much attention to the state of repair of the rest houses. In one rest house there was an entry by Chief Commissioner Armstrong about a leaking roof, saying 'If the political neophyte will look around he will see that the natives re-roof their houses every year'. The political neophyte in this year before World War I was one Mr Rake who retired before World War II, but returned during the war for a tour.

Another enquiry which was assigned to me was in the West of Ashanti, where a village and surrounding area comprising about 2000 people wanted their own local authority. I always had some sympathy with a small community wishing to run their own affairs, but I had to recommend refusal in this case. I posed the problem of financing such a small local authority. I felt sure they would have some difficulty in answering that one, but they were quite undaunted. They pointed to some hills and said 'There is gold in those hills over there'. I suggested that it was surprising that nobody was mining it, but once again they were undaunted – its location was a secret only known to them. It was an interesting incursion into the world of make-believe, but perhaps the chances of finding gold were about equal to those of winning the National Lottery in Britain today.

I was on leave between March and August, 1954. For me personally the most important event took place in May when I had to convey Faith to Townlands Hospital in Henley to give birth to William, our second son. My leave was much concerned with our house and garden and provided good exercise and much enjoyment. In the Gold Coast an election was held in June which gave the CPP a resounding victory in an election for a constitution designed to prepare for independence in December, 1956. Things did not work out quite like that, but in Africa the unexpected was always quite commonplace.

CHAPTER XIV

Turmoil on the Way
to Independence

THE ELECTIONS OF JUNE, 1954, provided a clear mandate from the country by means of direct elections for Kwame Nkrumah's CPP. His party won 79 out of 104 seats with the only opposition of any consequence coming from the NPP (Northern Peoples Party). which won 14 seats. This opposition was, however, more important than it appeared in that indirectly it encouraged the growth of the NLM (National Liberation Movement) based largely upon Ashanti. Thus soon after the election there came to be some substantial regional opposition to the CPP. This was also present in Togoland where the Togo Unionists were active. There were political differences between the CPP and the NPP over attitudes to tradition and chieftainship. There was greater reverence towards these matters in Ashanti too, but the problem was mainly an economic one. Much of the country's wealth came from cocoa, particularly the Ashanti crop, but the farmers saw little personal benefit from high world prices. The benefits were largely channelled into higher export taxes and the Cocoa Marketing Board. This wealth was seen as being used in southern areas for development there, which added to the honour and glory of the CPP. Although the Northern Territories did not produce cocoa there was a feeling that the region should not be left out of the prosperity of the country as a whole. There grew up a regionalism which the CPP dubbed tribalism in an attempt to get over their discomfort. The regional divisions were the cause of worry for Sir Charles Arden-Clarke and the Colonial Office; both would have preferred a steady approach to a unitary state with only token opposition to the ruling party.

When I returned from leave in August, 1954, there was much talk amongst friends and colleagues about the future of the Colonial Service. It was quite clear that things were changing rapidly and there was a large question mark over whether there was any future career in the Gold Coast or, indeed, anywhere in the British Empire. This was, perhaps surprisingly, not a source of gloom, as there was a general confidence that we would be fairly treated. There were precedents in India and the Sudan for compensation for loss of careers and it was generally expected that these precedents would be followed. The Colonial Office had not been specifically concerned in these cases, but the Colonial Office had generally been a good employer. There had been some tardiness in considering conditions arising from inflation during and after the war, but this had eventually been remedied with some back dating, which gave us all a welcome windfall in 'back pay'. The term went into widespread use in the Gold Coast and all and sundry sought it – cooks, garden boys, night watchmen and 'tankas men', who emptied thunder boxes in the morning.

The latter days were brightened by some humorists amongst us, who were worth their weight in gold in helping to maintain morale in the service, which remained remarkably high considering it was clearly in its latter days. Robin Blair was one of the foremost amongst those who looked for humour wherever it could be found and there were indeed plenty of opportunities; these only needed someone of his wit. He started his career as Assistant DC in Cape Coast in 1949 and an opportunity for exercising his humour came within a day or two. As often happened, induction into the art of administration was a chancy affair. Robin found himself on his own in the office when the telephone rang. He found the caller was one Topper Brown, who was an Assistant Superintendent with the Police Reserve Unit (the Riot Squad) stationed in Elmina Castle. It seems that Topper Brown had asked if he could be supplied with some paper clips, but someone – another humorist – had left a message offering some runcible flanges. Robin had no knowledge of the previous message, but found himself under police questioning over the nature of these flanges. He started his administrative career with the poem quoted below left on a colleague's desk; he also brought the word 'runcibilia' into use and described situations from which he could extract a little fun as a piece of runcibilia. The poem starting it all ran as follows:

Re Runcible Flanges, Topper Brown
Rang up to ask (with a puzzled frown)
If we knew what they were, for he hadn't a clue.
I wasn't quite sure and referred him to you.
Are they the ones with a sliding spline
And a goose-neck clutch on the central tine?
So fill up with petrol and prime it with tea
And whatever you do never point it at me;
Connect it in parallel, socket to ball,
And up will go Topper, Elmina and all.

I am sure Edward Lear would have approved, Robin was a man with a high degree of ability as well as a sense of fun. After Independence in the Gold Coast he was one of the few who managed to get accepted by the Commonwealth Relations Office, later amalgamated with the Foreign Office. He served in London and in India, but sadly he died at an early age. Whether he would have reached the higher ranks might have depended upon how far his sense of humour was diplomatically acceptable in somewhat more serious minded circles; it probably would have been appreciated by most in the service.

In the Regional Office in Cape Coast Bill Hope and Donald Kilbourn were colleagues who ensured that life was never dull. Bill might perhaps have missed his vocation as an actor, as he had a facility for impersonation and mimicry. Donald had some delightful expressions. When confronted by some surprising or annoying situation he used to say 'I will go hopping sideways to hell'. The meaning was never quite clear to me, but I laughed every time I heard it. Sometimes at the end of the morning on a Saturday, which marked the end of the working week, I used to go shopping with Donald. On one occasion he said that his wife, Sheila, had asked him to go to the UTC (Union Trading Company of Basle) to get a pot for his infant daughter; there were three young Swiss trainees there and I understood later why Sheila thought it a little embarrassing to go to get this item of toiletry. Donald duly asked for a pot for a child saying a diameter of eight inches was required. The first of the Swiss lads shouted to one Hans saying Mr Kilbourn wants a chamber pot. Hans then climbed a ladder bringing down a cascade of enamel items from the shelves, but eventually waved a pot triumphantly from the top shelf saying 'This one is twenty centimetres'. Conversion from inches to centimetres was something which baffled us both at the time, but for me eight inches

being about twenty centimetres became something of a yardstick
that I could remember. We both went to present Donald's
purchase to Sheila, who entertained me with some thirst
quenching Club Beer (an excellent Gold Coast beer). Before
Faith joined me later in the year I received much kindness from
Sheila and Donald and their friendship happily continued after
the Colonial days. The same applied in the case of Margaret
and Bill Hope; the latter worked with me in BAT for some
years and we enjoyed discussing past times and Ghanaian
matters as they evolved.

Cape Coast
Town Hall

The Town Hall in Cape Coast was the scene of various kinds
of entertainment. The Gold Coast Legion dance was an annual
affair and one occasion Bill and I were in charge of the takings
at the bar. Although adequate warning was given of the closure
of the bar, when we had added up all the cash we found a large
mob outside claiming a refund on their glasses for which they
had deposited one shilling. We decided they were too late but
had to make our way out through the window like bookies
escaping from angry punters at a race meeting. On another
occasion I had to make a more embarrassing escape through a
window. I was with Barry Lane when as the police officer in
charge in Cape Coast he was informed that there was a riot in
the Town Hall. This turned out to be a minor protest at a film

show. Barry settled the matter very easily by stamping his foot on the stage, rather like my old headmaster, and demanding silence which was immediately achieved. I had a slight problem in that I needed to visit the 'Gents', but it was locked. Barry said I should use the 'Ladies', adding 'nobody will bother here'. I duly did this, but found to my horror when I had shut the door that the handle on the lock on the door was missing. I just managed to get out through the small window much to Barry's amusement. Fortunately, the local press did not get hold of the story. They would have loved to report 'Judicial Adviser escapes from Ladies lavatory'. The press were somewhat hostile to the administration, but it is fair to say that the reporters were generally good humoured about it and less vindictive in criticizing than some of the British press today. For Barry the affair in the Town Hall was a very minor incident. Early in his police career he had been with Colin Imray at the crossroads in the Accra riots in 1948. He also had a frightening experience when he was in charge of the Mobile Force in Elmina Castle as one of his very young sons fell out of a window high up in the castle. Surprisingly and fortunately he was only slightly injured and shocked as he fell in the old sand filled moat. A constable jumped fifteen feet off the old drawbridge to rescue the lad, who had fallen from more than twice that height.

My work became increasingly a matter of helping DCs and others to keep all their activities as strictly as possible within the law in the midst of much political criticism of DCs. I tried to continue with the process of widening the membership of Native Court panels and training Registrars, but there was a Commission appointed under Mr Justice Korsah to consider the future of Native Courts. In my view there was no need for any great changes. The name needed to be changed to Local Courts and there needed to be wider representation on the panels. John Matson as substantive SJA was a member of the Commission and my views were not officially sought, although John Matson knew them and I think in general agreed. However, the eventual conclusion was that there should be lay magistrates sitting singly to constitute the courts. This I regarded as about the worst solution in making the possibilities of corruption greater than ever before; there was also the probability of getting appointees without much knowledge of customary law in the particular place concerned. The panel system was, however, continuing to cause me some difficulties when there were two political factions as in Akim Abuakwa, where the court was sitting in two divisions. In Kibi the older traditional members were sitting as they always had done without Kibi having been declared as a place of sitting. There was an argument for saying that I should have intervened by reviewing cases heard in Kibi and setting aside the judgments. In my view, however, the question was one which could best be settled on appeal, but nobody had appealed and there was apparent satisfaction in the area with the situation. Briefly, I did not consider it to be right to exercise powers of review when the ordinary appellate procedure was available. The CPP Ministers took a different view, so I was subjected to a certain amount of pressure from the Ministry of Local Government in Accra. This did not worry me unduly, but it gave me a clue regarding the direction in which the future of an administrative job in the Gold Coast was moving.

We did not have to wait long for a statement on the future of the Colonial Service in the Gold Coast. When the expected circular came it stated that from an operative date in July, 1955, the Secretary of State would cease to have any responsibility for the service in the Gold Coast, which would become a local civil service. There was a clear statement on lump sum compensation for loss of career, which immediately became known as 'lumpers'. The maximum was £8,000 payable at the age of 39 years. The scale rose in steps to this age and then fell away as the normal age of retirement was approached. The scheme also provided for pensions to be paid after ten years service based upon retirement salary. The sum of £8,000 in 1955 was a substantial one which was enough for the purchase of two houses such as the one I had recently bought in England. The scheme made it plain that the choice was one for the individual, but there was a certain amount of talk by some persons about having a duty to see the Gold Coast through into independence; most of this was bogus and misconceived. Each individual had to consider his own position and it was to the credit of the Governor and the Colonial Office that fair terms were set out at an early stage. Many redundancy arrangements in Britain today could learn much from the straightforward way in which this matter was handled. It was perhaps unfortunate that a division tended to develop between those staying after the operative date and those going. The division was exacerbated by a decision to send everyone who had decided to go off on the first boat after the operative date; the term the 'rats' boat' was quite quickly adopted by those staying.

Deciding what to do was difficult for everyone. For me the question was relatively simple as I was in the fortunate position of being near the maximum compensation. I was also about two years below the age of forty, which was sometimes a cut-off point at that time for eligibility for jobs. The question of owing a duty to the service after the operative date did not seem to me to arise. I was appointed to HM Overseas Civil Service (as it became known), but after the operative date the Secretary of State was relinquishing his responsibilities. There was a general feeling in the service of duty towards the ordinary citizens of the Gold Coast, but for the future their welfare was going to be in the hands of their own politicians who were promising great things for them. We may have felt they were being duped, but we were powerless to do anything about it.

The fact that there was so much discussion about duty might perhaps show the service to have been one with a strong sense of it. A suggestion, however, made to one of my colleagues that we had a duty to the Commonwealth was taking things much too far verging on the ludicrous. I first heard that it had been made on one of my visits to Accra, when I was staying with Rodney Bennett. The idea led us to start a little parody on a song from *HMS Pinafore*, the well known Gilbert and Sullivan opera. The chorus lines ran:

> He's a duty to the Commonwealth,
> He has put aside all thought of self,
> That is why he is going to stay
> Until inde-inde-inde-inde-inde-independence Day.

The rest of the parody of 'He is an Englishman' was made up later by a number of artists. I am not sure who they all were, but I do not doubt that Robin Blair the runcible poet had a hand in it. He had a strong sense of duty, but also a great sense of fun.

The compensation scheme was designed to encourage as many expatriates as possible to stay on for a while. This encouragement was minimal for someone of my age. More senior officers nearing retirement age could freeze their compensation at the figure at which it stood on the operative date and carry on with the prospect of an increasing pension. Younger officers had of course the prospect of increasing compensation. Brian Smith who was my Regional Officer at the time told me that he would stay until the flag came down on Independence Day. He said I was foolish as I had been recommended for promotion. I did not know this, but I had realized it was probable and had taken account of it. However, I reckoned it would cause a delay of a year or two in getting another job in Britain and it was not a suitable course to take; I could hardly accept promotion and then resign. Brian asked me to stay until October instead of going on the operative date and this I readily agreed to do. Faith was joining me in May with William, aged one year, and Nigel could come for his summer holiday. For once Faith and I could travel home together.

It was perhaps ironical that as far as Faith and I were concerned our happiest time in the Gold Coast seemed to be in the months

Bungalow No. 6 at
Cape Coast

A Sunday morning
haircut for Nigel

immediately before we left. We were in Bungalow No. 6 which
in former days had been the residence of Provincial Commissioners. It was a large wooden bungalow on stilts which now
had mosquito proofed bedrooms at each end. There was an
enclosed verandah on which William could sleep and be heard
if he needed anything without being disturbed by us. Faith was
able to do a few hours teaching each day at the Holy Child
College whilst Paul Kweku and the rest of the domestic staff
capably looked after William, which I think they enjoyed doing.
Silas Bortey was very reliable in taking Faith and William
anywhere when I was not available. As well as being a good
driver Bortey was a man who made himself well known in the
neighbourhood. On one occasion when he was driving Faith
he waved to a lady on the roadside and remarked cheerfully
'that was my old wife'. Faith quickly realized that the term
'old' was used meaning 'former', as she was an attractive young
girl.

From the point of view of my work I was gradually becoming
less happy with what was happening. The Akim Abuakwa court
was coming into the foreground again. I kept getting telephone
calls from John Duncan and others telling me that the Minister
(Local Government) wanted to know why some members of
the court were continuing to sit in Kibi and why I was not

doing anything to stop them; one such call which particularly annoyed me came on a Saturday afternoon when I was about to get into the car to take Faith and William to the beach. I tried to explain that the court had to settle its own affairs and if members sitting in Kibi were acting unlawfully this was something best settled by way of an appeal against a judgment. I did not blame John Duncan or anyone else for making the calls, but they showed me how little I should have liked a job in a Ministry with a political Minister.

It was not long before I was summoned to Accra to give an account of my refusal to exercise my powers of review over cases heard in Kibi. There I found myself required to answer this question before the Prime Minister, Kwame Nkrumah, and the Minister of Local Government Asafu Adjaye. The Ministers were supported by the Attorney General, Mr Forbes, who said he did not think there was any doubt that the court sitting in Kibi was an illegal one. The Ministers, therefore, took the simplistic view that I should exercise my powers to review all cases heard there. Happily Donald Hardy, who was acting as Regional Officer of the Eastern Region at the time, was also present. Here I had a friend who shared my view and he was not one to be shaken off what he believed to be right by political expediency. He was not called upon to say much, but it was a great source of strength to have him there. My first task was to get acceptance from the Attorney General of my contention that there could be two views on the question of legality of the court and that the proper place for a decision on that was in the higher courts. He did not like it, but as a fellow member of the bar, although in a higher office, he had to accept it. The Ministers were somewhat non-plussed by the collapse of their case, but I went on to insist that Prime Minister, Nkrumah, should confirm that he understood my position. This, to his credit, he did. The case was much more complex than they had thought. I could well have been wrong in arguing that the court might not be illegal, but in any event it would have been wrong to upset judgments accepted by the parties concerned by an administrative act.

Donald and I betook ourselves to the Accra Club and discussed the mornings proceeding over a bottle or two of beer; it had been thirsty work. We both agreed that the position we had maintained would become increasingly difficult as the country moved to independence. Happily Faith and I remained in touch with Donald and Carol when he was the parish priest in two parishes near Cambridge. They did me the honour of asking me to be god-father to one of their younger sons born after they left the Gold Coast. It was extremely unlikely that I could do anything to enhance his godliness, but it is pleasant to have this type of link with a younger generation. John Hardy is now a parish priest in Newcastle and it is a happy thing to be in touch with him as well as his mother. Sadly Donald died some twenty years ago.

Domestic and social life in Cape Coast continued largely in the old colonial style. However, there were changes for the better in that there were more Africans in senior positions and thus in the social circle. This helped to lead parties away from some of the boring old discussions of previous tours in various parts of the country, the office files and Elder Dempster voyages. Faith always tried to make parties in our house slightly different in arranging some form of afterdinner activity. Carpet bowls was quite a popular game, although our carpet was rather small for it. A rompier activity was obstacle racing through the dining room chairs, which was a testing activity for stouter members of any party. However we never sent anyone home permanently attached to a chair.

The Brian Smiths held some pleasant, but more staid parties at Government Lodge. On one occasion when we were going there Faith sent a pleated skirt for the 'washman' to press. Unfortunately, this fat jolly man usually to be seen covered in soapsuds did not understand the niceties of a pleated skirt and it came back after much effort had been put into it with the pleats pressed out. It was my task to get Paul to return the skirt to the washman with instructions to replace the pleats. Sadly the skirt came back very quickly with a statement that washman says 'so he be'. There was really no room for argument, or anything other than laughter and making the best of an unpleated skirt. After we left the Gold Coast we heard from Paul, our cook and general factotum until he died in 1991. One of the earlier letters sent us greetings from others whom Paul had seen and ended with the charming words 'washman is waving his hands to you'. The washmen were an interesting breed often from Ewe country. They plied their trade around various households as independent contractors who negotiated with cooks and stewards for employment. They believed in a copious use of soap and for some reason Key Soap was preferred; long bars of it did not last very long. The first wash of garments of clothing on return to Britain often revealed where much of the soap had remained; rinsing things out well was not a strong point amongst Gold Coast washmen.

Amongst friends in Cape Coast with whom we have kept in touch were Ian and Molly Cochran and Stewart Lawson. There was often discussion about what we might do after leaving the Colonial Service. This often bore little relation to what actually happened. As Molly was a Nursing Sister before her marriage she and Ian made quite a natural progression to running a Nursing Home in Edinburgh. Ian later took to teaching and he did me the honour of asking me to give him a reference when applying for a job. The school in Edinburgh was interested in how far he might help with sporting activities and I remember writing how he had introduced cricket to Enchi and set up a golf course in Mpraeso. I do not know the reaction, but he got the job. Stewart also continued his career in Scotland, firstly in the family business and later in the golfing world as a leading member of the Royal and Ancient in St Andrews. I have already mentioned that Bill Hope joined me in BAT. Donald Kilbourn also had a proxy association with BAT through joining Wiggins Teape, which was a company acquired by BAT. He also spent some time in a tannery, but later went into consultancy work and has now married a widow and betaken himself with her to France. Before that he and Sheila until she died were living in Norfolk in an area apparently below sea level. There could be a conclusion that members of the service were versatile people, but perhaps we should be called Jacks of all trades.

A happy thing about the latter colonial days was the forma-tion of life-long friendships. I still enjoyed trying to help DCs and others with legal tangles arising from rapidly changing legislation and circumstances; there were plenty of politically minded people ready to pounce on mistakes, so getting things right first time was very important. There was political turmoil arising from increasing militancy amongst Ashantis. There were explosions in various parts of Kumasi, which did little damage but gave rise to some unease. The explosive used was generally gunpowder which when contained in an empty petrol tin could make a very loud noise. The Governor was not very popular in Kumasi and at one time had stones thrown at his car. On a visit to Cape Coast he told an afterdinner story of how an

'Consuls at Sunset'. One of the last uniformed gatherings for the wedding of Rodney and Elizabeth Bennett

audience with the Queen had been relieved of any tension, as she had asked him about the stoning of his car and laughed at his account of it. He held a meeting with DCs from the Western Region in the course of his visit to Cape Coast. As usual he was very frank about his problems with politicians and said that unfortunately their attitude to any opposition was to look for the biggest stick they could find to beat them down. He was not particularly optimistic about the future of local government, but he took up a question that I asked about training for local government staff. I had in mind something along the lines of what I had been doing for native court registrars. However, to my great surprise shortly afterwards a local government school was set up in Accra under the charge of Bernard Bumpus, an Ashanti DC Bernard was a very pleasant man, who at one stage had his mother to stay with him for a time. She inevitably became known as Ma Bump. Some of the dignity and ceremony of the old colonial days was recaptured at the wedding in Accra of Rodney and Elizabeth Bennett in June, 1955. The bridegroom was married in the Colonial Service uniform and friends including myself formed an arch with our swords outside the Ridge Church in Accra. It was the last occasion on which I donned my uniform and a very happy memory. It is also very pleasant to see Rodney and Elizabeth over forty years later. At the time the day provided a welcome relief from day to day politics with which we tended to become obsessed. Rodney aptly named a photograph 'Consuls at Sunset'.

The system of Native Courts was to be abolished in favour of single lay magistrates, so my work in this direction lost interest for me. The plan was that when I left Ron Woolley would take over the winding up of the old system working in the Ministry

A shunting engine in Takoradi harbour

of Local Government in Accra. This job would have appalled me, particularly as I had happily avoided having to work in the Secretariat or a Ministry for the whole of my time in the Gold Coast. I might have been promoted to another job but it would almost certainly have been in a Ministry.

Domestically life was happier than it had been and Faith and I both felt our servants as an extension of our family. We were very sad when the time came in October to leave them. We were of course sorry to leave all our British friends, but we had the feeling in that case that we would be able to see them again in the UK. The Brian Smiths gave a party for us before we left. They had always been very kind to us and Faith was particularly touched by the trouble Margaret took to get some water to her, which she needed badly for William, when the Cape Coast water supply failed owing to very heavy rainfall flooding the waterworks. At the party to see us off Bill Hope and Christopher Paton made up a little song mostly about my eccentricities, but with the pleasing note that DCs around the country did like ringing me up for advice or reassurance. I had known both Bill and Christopher for a long time. Christopher took over our house and the curtains which were inherited from the days of the Burners, who originally had some pelmets looking like brassieres. I met Christopher quite frequently later in London when he was Warden of International Students House.

Both Faith and I travelled to Takoradi with heavy hearts. For my part I felt a sense of failure in that I seemed to be leaving a country not ready for self-government; my recent work was unfinished and unlikely to be finished in the way I had envisaged. Faith had a very appreciative farewell from the girls of the Holy Child where at least the work was continuing. The girls gave her a lamp of African wood carved in the shape of an elephant; this has illuminated much of my present writing. The staff sent some gold ear-rings to greet her on the boat at Takoradi, where we were cheered by other friends seeing us off. These included Buck (Buckley) my Customs and Excise friend in Togoland, who was now in charge of Customs at the port of Takoradi. We were in any event unlikely to have met any problems with Customs, although we had a number of packing cases made of Odum wood; the export of this wood had recently been prohibited to preserve stocks for the Gold Coast, as it is a very hard wood resistant to white ants (termites).

We boarded the *Aureol,* the third and last of the post-war

Elder Dempster ships to be built. The idea was to run a fortnightly service based on three ships, but this did not continue for long as air travel became increasingly used. The travelling time was eventually thus reduced from thirteen days to twelve or thirteen hours. In some ways it was unfortunate that sea travel gradually declined as the sea journey home generally seemed good for health after continuous living in tropical heat and the return journey gave time to come to terms with working again after four months leave. The *Aureol* was the first Elder Dempster ship to be provided with a nursery for young children. However, we found this was not very suitable for an eighteen-months-old child, as it was dominated by four and five-year-old children. All went well, however, until the last night when William had a cold. He went to sleep quite quickly and we went to dinner, but, alas, the Liverpool Pilot Boat came alongside and let off its siren right outside our cabin. There was also the noise of the anchor being let down, and that was the end of sleep for the night; we were hardly amused when a steward came in and said very apologetically that the people next door had said there was a child crying. We appreciated their point, but our parental ingenuity was by that time completely exhausted.

The Gold Coast moved somewhat uneasily to Independence on the 6th March, 1957. It had been intended that Independence should come at the end of 1956, but problems over the Ashanti desire for a federal constitution prevented this. The NLM gained strength in 1955 and it was necessary to have another election in the middle of 1956, so that the National Assembly could be representative of the state of the parties at the time of Independence; it had been intended that the election of 1954 would set the pattern for Independence. Attempts by Sir Frederick Bourne to mediate in the dispute between the CPP and Ashanti did not produce any tangible results. The election of July, 1956, gave the CPP 72 seats out of 104, which was a substantial majority in the country as a whole, but the NLM obtained 12 seats in Ashanti against 8 for the CPP and the Northern Peoples Party (NPP) obtained 15 seats in the North against 11 for the CPP. Quite a strong force could therefore, be mustered in favour of a federal constitution; there was also the point that the Colony, Ashanti and the Northern Territories had each become part of a British Colonial Territory under separate arrangements. There was another complication over Togoland in that the Togo Congress and the CPP were in disagreement over its future; the CPP wanted continuation of the existing unification with the Gold Coast, whereas the Togo Congress wanted to be associated with French Togoland in an All-Ewe country. A plebiscite was held in May, 1956, and a substantial majority – a little less than two thirds – voted for integration with the Gold Coast. The Brong-Amafo people in Northern Ashanti were also a complication in that they had never regarded themselves as properly part of Ashanti. Eventually a visit by Lennox Boyd (later Lord Boyd) was arranged for early in 1957. The visit was opposed for some time by Nkrumah, but eventually he agreed and a settlement was reached based on a unified constitution. This enabled the Union Flag to be lowered and the Black Star of Ghana to be raised on the 6th March, 1957, one hundred and thirteen years after the Bond of 1844 from which British rule dated over part of the Gold Coast. This took place at an impressive midnight ceremony at which the Queen was represented by the Duchess of Kent. Ghana became one of the Queen's Dominions and later it became a Republic within the Commonwealth, but that and later events are not part of this book.

CHAPTER XV

Reflections in Retrospect

W HEN I LEFT the Gold Coast I felt a sense of failure in
that we British were leaving the country with our tasks
unfinished. I did not know what I was going to do for a future
career, although I had a number of ideas in mind. Without
really expecting anything to happen I made contact with the
Oxford University Appointments Board. I thought they would
think they had finished with me when they had paved my way
into the Colonial Service. On the contrary I found a most
helpful attitude and after an interview I received a note about
a job in the Personnel Department of British-American Tobacco
Company (BAT), which was looking for someone with experience in Africa. Never having been a smoker or had any interest
in the tobacco industry I did not expect much to come of an
application for the post. However, to my surprise I was appointed and served the Company for the next seventeen years,
being concerned with Africa for the first six years and Asia
thereafter.

The job in BAT gave me the opportunity to visit various
parts of Africa, which led me to the conclusion a few years later
that in the Gold Coast we had done as good a job in bringing
about independence as had been done anywhere in the Continent. Ghana had led the way in Africa and my visits there
surprised me in finding that things were working so well. I
came to the conclusion that we had taught better than I had
thought; former clerks had moved quite easily into becoming
Government Agents (the successors of DCs).

For various reasons, including the lack of a community of
white settlers and a relatively short sea journey to Europe, the
West African Colonies were probably the most advanced in
Africa towards self-government. During my army career I had
seen something of Nigeria and Sierra Leone and when the
French territories ceased to be potentially hostile I saw a little
of their administration. This was in many respects similar to
that in British West African Colonies, but the objective was to
make them part of a greater France rather than set them up as
self-governing countries. However, the latter was fairly easily

achievable once Ghana had shown the way. There was, however, more direct French influence after independence. This did not apply to Guinea, where Sekoue Toure had the audacity to say '*non*' to General de Gaulle, whereas the other colonies agreed to the loose form of association which he offered.

Amongst British Colonies the Gold Coast was well placed to lead the way to independence, as it had less tribal rivalry than some colonies. Nigeria was so large that it inevitably had greater problems with different ethnic groups; there was a well-established Muslim political system in the North, whilst the economic prosperity was in the South. Here again there was some disparity between the Yorubas and the relatively poor, but intelligent, Ibos. Sierra Leone and The Gambia were much smaller colonies and much less prosperous than the Gold Coast, which derived its economic progress from cocoa, gold, manganese and timber. Another important factor was the personality and competence as a politician of Kwame Nkrumah, who was able both to stir up popular opinion in his favour and at the same time make himself acceptable to the British Governor, Sir Charles Arden-Clarke. It could also be said, put the other way round that Nkrumah was fortunate to have a man of Arden-Clarke's experience and also adaptability to a changing world.

In East Africa the colonial scene differed from that in West Africa and there were also important differences between the colonies of Kenya, Uganda and Tanganyika. They were all under a British administration on the same basis as West African colonies, but the presence of white settlers in Kenya had a great influence on that colony and to a lesser extent upon the other two. Another important influence was the presence of Asian immigrants, who had come in large numbers when the railways were built. They were regarded as a source of semi-skilled labour for this work and were expected to go back to India when the work was finished. However, many remained and became small traders or artisans such as carpenters and mechanics. This slowed down the formation of an African middle class, which developed in West Africa. There was thus a less viable society on a purely African basis.

The biggest mistake made regarding East Africa was the settlement of lands in the highlands of Kenya by white persons mostly from Britain after World War I. The highlands reaching 6000 feet or more had a climate in which Europeans could live, in spite of being near the equator. The mistake arose mainly from thinking that large sparsely inhabited lands did not belong to anybody. They were Kikuyu lands and the friction arising from the European takeover led eventually to the Mau Mau campaign against white people. Personally I felt at home in the old East African colonies except in Nairobi and the white dominated area around it. Here I found an artificial atmosphere where there was racial disharmony going beyond anything I had met elsewhere. When I told a lady at a Nairobi cocktail party, where only the servants were black, that I was going to Mwanza in Tanganyika on the next day she looked on me with pity and said 'Do you have to go?'. Happily she slid away somewhere else quite quickly after I said I was looking forward to it.

My biggest surprise in travelling around Africa came when I visited the Belgian Congo. On my first visit before Independence I was amazed to see the Customs shed almost entirely staffed by Belgians. I realized quite soon that the country was run by Belgians for Belgians as an annexe of Belgium. Whereas agriculture in British West Africa had remained in the hands of Africans in the Belgian Congo there were large European managed plantations. There were very few Africans with a professional or university education, but events elsewhere in Africa had not gone unnoticed and there were political parties forming. By 1960 the Belgians decided it was time to grant independence; they seemed to be hoping that things could carry on much as before with law and order being maintained by a Belgian officered Force Publique. This was an efficient body for dealing with riots, but it only took about two weeks after Independence for the members to mutiny against their Belgian officers. This led to the force taking the law into its own hands with a resulting pillage in many towns and some raping of wives of the Belgian officers. The United Nations sent in forces to re-establish law and order using troops and police from other African countries. This achieved a fair degree of success, but internal wars and general disorder became part of life in the Congo.

I saw some of the disarray of the country on my next visit. I arrived in Leopoldville (Kinshasha) to find a scene of general disorganization at the airport. I was eventually able to get out of the Customs and Immigration shed to be met by Peter Rombaut the BAT man in Leopoldville. He was anxious about getting me into town before the midnight curfew and also about getting me a 'laissez passer' for my journey to Stanleyville

(Kisangani) on the next day. The latter was achieved by Peter dictating what had to be written to a clerk in an office and getting an official to put a stamp on it. Thereafter my journey to Stanleyville where the Company had its main operations was achieved without let or hindrance. At the Stanleyville airport I was met by Bob Clark, but he was unable to persuade the vaccinator that my smallpox certificate showed the required vaccination within one year. It seemed that the vaccinator charged whatever he thought fit for a vaccination and put any excess over the government charge in his pocket.

Things proceeded fairly smoothly until the Sunday morning, a day or two before I was booked to return to Leopoldville. Then like everyone in town with a white face I was arrested together with Bob Clark. We were taken to the hotel in the town where we had to join a queue to have our documents checked. Bob's papers did not cause any trouble, as he had locally issued and understood papers, but my British passport baffled the officer in charge. An Ethiopian United Nations officer came and asked whether I had any problem. When I explained the position to him he suggested that I should get in touch with my consul, but there was not one in Stanleyville. However, this set me thinking that there should be a consul, and I made a mental note to do something about it. Eventually after waiting for the rest of the morning in the hotel, where happily Bob and I were allowed to order a drink, I was given a note written on the back of a Martell Brandy advertisement. It said that I was '*en congé*' in the Congo. I managed to make a rather feeble joke about the *congé* (holiday in my French) with the officer concerned and we parted good friends. It struck me that one of the problems the Belgians had in the Congo was a lack of rapport with the Congolese. It seemed to me that they could be as friendly as Africans elsewhere if treated with ordinary good manners in a friendly fashion. The situation in Stanleyville was the antithesis of this and highly dangerous with a large number of ill-trained men going around with guns; they never gave the impression of wanting to shoot anyone, but I did not know how much they knew about the safety catches on their rifles.

When back in Leopoldville I went to see the British Ambassador and gave him an account of events in Stanleyville. I told him that I understood the local administrator, Salumu, planned to hold similar '*ratisages*' from time to time. I had learnt this as when enquiring what to do about documents for me to leave

Stanleyville, Bob had been told that I should wait until the next *ratisage*; happily I did not have to do this. The Ambassador started by suggesting that I was perhaps like others coming from outside unduly alarmed by events in the Congo. I was soon able to assure him that I had spent sixteen years in Africa and I had never seen anything else that could be called really alarming. To my surprise some months later, whether because of my representation or for other reasons, the Foreign Office sent a young diplomat from the United States to Stanleyville.

Events in the Congo showed what could happen in a country granted self-government with completely inadequate training and preparation for it. In some ways Portuguese colonies were similar, but in Angola I noticed a much greater rapport between the Portuguese and the Angolans than existed between the Belgians and the Congolese. Angola was in many ways a less developed country outside the capital Luanda, but in the bush there were Portuguese living as smallholders beside Africans in a similar situation. There were also some baronial style Portuguese living in the bush in much more palatial buildings. In one place I visited, a Portuguese gentleman lived in a large house built around a courtyard with quarters for his retainers; it struck me at the time that some of these seemed to be attractive young ladies. Living conditions for travellers outside Luanda were somewhat uncomfortable with beds designed rather like the rough roads, primitive toilet facilities, inedible food and un-drinkable beer. I thought sardines should be good in a Portuguese country, but they had been drowned in some very unusual oil. I have usually found Portuguese people easy to relate to on a friendly basis, but I was unfortunate to visit Angola at a time when India had recently invaded Goa. I spent an uncomfortable time listening to a tirade from a Portuguese lady about how we British had stood idly by, although we were their oldest ally. The Portuguese regarded their empire wherever it was as part of Portugal; Angola was of course no exception to this.

My visits to other parts of Africa made me feel happier about British achievements in the Gold Coast than I had been when I left. My later travels in former colonial territories in the Far East also made me happier. I particularly remember just two remarks which I thought very interesting at the time. One was by a member of Nehru family in India, who said referring to his country, 'We were very lucky to have had the British'. Then in Indonesia where things were in some turmoil after the

Soekarno regime an American member of their Embassy said in a charming southern accent 'Where the British have been you can live like a human being.'.

A retrospective view of the years I spent in the Gold Coast has given me the feeling that we can compare quite well with the colonial effort anywhere. That does not mean we did not make mistakes; there were many. Some were fundamental long term failings of policy, and amongst these a failure to have any idea of the time available for preparing for self-government was perhaps the most serious. We tended to regard self-government as something to be achieved in unlimited time. Another failure was in the manner in which we applied indirect rule over much of the country. The principle was right and worked very well in Northern Nigeria and to a lesser extent in the Northern Territories of the Gold Coast, but these areas had well established chiefly rule. In the more southern parts of the Gold Coast, particularly in the Colony, we did not really understand the nature of rule by chiefs. For a long time we tended to regard chiefs as having more power than they wielded. We tended to think a Chief who said he would have to consult his Elders as playing for time, whereas the Elders did exercise real power. We also tried to keep Chiefs on their Stools when they had become unpopular.

The system of chiefly rule was perhaps more democratic than we realized. Sir Alan Burns wrote in strong terms about the disadvantages of Stool Disputes and partly as a result we tended to try to protect chiefs by a system of charges having to be set out before a chief could be destooled. According to custom destoolment was more often effected by a hue and cry and general disorder outside the Ahinfie; thereafter when the situation became too hot for him the chief threw off his sandals and fled. The next problem was electing a new chief with the Queen Mother being the prime mover in this, but movement was often slow. There was some very erudite research done into the system by R. S. Rattray in the nineteen thirties, but this particularly referred to Ashanti. Also as far as Ashanti was concerned my colleague John Matson wrote a simple handbook for DCs. Such a work would also have been most useful for other parts of the country; the Ewe areas particularly come to mind, as here the customs were quite different.

Other matters over which we found it difficult to come to terms with African customs were over customary gifts and sexual mores. We had great difficulty in distinguishing between customary gifts and bribes and over sexual mores the Christian missions exercised considerable influence. I do not by any means denigrate the dedicated work of the missions, but I think they might have been less condemnatory in some instances. It is perhaps interesting to note that in Britain today we seem to have lapsed in both these matters. Our sexual mores are certainly nearer to those of Africa; I do not know of anything along the lines of the jolly dance, but there probably is something.

It is interesting to consider whether there are any lessons to be learnt from the last days of the Colonial Service in the Gold Coast and elsewhere in Africa. Perhaps one thing not universally understood is that you cannot judge an African situation by comparison with our own accepted principles. It is particularly dangerous to regard regimes on the basis of our democratic principles. There are different concepts of democracy and also of corrupt practices in different places. Support for a regime or support for opposition to a regime can too easily have the opposite effect of that intended. A dictator can gain strength by suggesting that he is being harassed by foreign enemies and sanctions tend to bear hardest upon the poorest.

Something that I regard as very good about the Colonial Service was the management of people in it. This was by no means always apparent at the time, but now I often think how much better the demise of the service was handled compared with many redundancy situations today. Basically the difference came in being taken into confidence at an early stage and informed what the terms would be. This may not always be commercially possible, but I think the whole question of the rapport between members of the service of widely differing seniority is worthy of note. In the commercial world I have been to quite a number of courses on management, but they mostly fail to get to the point of the essential need for trust between members of the organization. There is much talk of team work. This was a term rarely used in the colonial service days unless there was a cricket match or something similar. We were, however, a team of undefined constitution with a strong sense of purpose; we did not use words such as goals and targets and now I avoid them except in their proper context. I regard myself as highly privileged to have served in the Gold Coast and elsewhere in Africa. We were supposedly in an educative role in the Colonial Service, but I am quite sure I learnt more than I ever taught anybody.

Historical Events Before 1939

Date

1469	Portuguese arrived at Elmina. Started trading with manufactured goods in exchange for gold.
1482	Stones, timber and other material brought from Portugal for the building of Elmina Castle. The slave trade was developing with the aid of local practices. Some slaves taken home to Portugal.
1497	Vasco da Gama sailed past West Africa and around the Cape of Good Hope to India.
1580	Portuguese and Spanish thrones united resulting in Portuguese becoming engaged in Spanish war with the Dutch.
1596	The Dutch attempted to capture Elmina. They failed, but later took the fort at Axim.
1637	Dutch captured Elmina. They also took some parts of Brazil from the Portuguese and continued the trade of taking slaves there. The Portuguese carried on their trade from Angola.
1664	Cape Coast Castle taken from the Dutch by the British. Thereafter it was known as the English castle. During the rest of the 17th Century, the Danish, Spanish, French and Swedish all joined in the slave trade.
1787	After centuries of slave trading more had become generally known about it and the Anti-Slavery Society was formed in Britain.
1807	The Wilberforce Act abolishing slavery by forbidding its practice was passed.
1817	The Dutch followed the British in passing a law against slavery.
1821	The Governor of Sierra Leone, Sir Charles MacCarthy, was appointed Governor of the Gold Coast Settlements.
1824	Sir Charles MacCarthy died whilst trying to end Ashanti dominance around the Castles and Forts.
1828	A Committee of Merchants was formed to administer funds provided by the Government for the Castles and Forts. This body was formed out of the Company of Merchants, which had been in charge of the Castles and Forts since 1750. The Governor of Sierra Leone remained nominally in charge.

1830   George Maclean appointed President of the Council of Merchants, which had been formed on the Gold Coast. By patient negotiation he achieved peace with Ashanti.

1836–38 George Maclean in Britain engaged upon negotiations over the future of the Gold Coast and also on leave. He married the authoress L. E. L. (Letitia Elizabeth Loudon). She returned to Cape Coast with him, but died soon after arrival. There was speculation whether she was poisoned, as she became ill and died very suddenly, but it is probably not necessary to look beyond illnesses such as malaria.

1840   The Madden report was severely critical of Maclean's failure to stamp out slavery amongst Africans themselves. He had little difficulty in pointing out that his powers did not extend beyond the Castles and Forts.

1844   The Castles and Forts were brought under Crown rule. George Maclean was appointed Judicial Assessor with jurisdiction over the Fanti tribes. On the 6th March a Bond was signed by the Fanti tribes. This became known as the Bond of 1844.

1847   George Maclean died. He had achieved much with few powers and sparse funds. In 1947 Thorlief Mangin (later Sir Thorlief) dedicated a plaque to him in Cape Coast Castle.

1863   First Ashanti War began and continued until 1864. The Ashantis were driven back over the Pra River. British troops suffered heavy losses from disease.

1872   The Dutch handed over Elmina Castle and all their properties to the British. The Danes had left in 1850, so from 1872 onwards the British were the only European power in the Gold Coast.

1873   Sir Garnet Wolseley was appointed Administrator and Commander in Chief and he set about driving the Ashantis back from the coast.

1874   Wolseley's troops reached Kumasi and sacked the town, but obtained no more than a renunciation of Ashanti claims to jurisdiction over coastal tribes.

1880   Brandford Griffith became Lieutenant Governor. He became Governor in 1886 and was in office until 1895. He followed a course of peaceful negotiation with the Ashantis and there was relative calm.

1895   Joseph Chamberlain became Secretary of State for the Colonies. He took an imperialistic view and instructed Maxwell, Griffith's successor, to bring the Ashantis under control. He led an expedition to Kumasi and brought the Asantehene to Elmina Castle and subsequently deported him to the Seychelles.

1900   Governor Hodgson, Maxwell's successor, was faced with an Ashanti uprising as a result of demanding the Golden Stool of Ashanti.

1901   Ashanti was annexed by Order in Council at the beginning of the reign of Edward VII. Governors following Hodgson adopted a more conciliatory approach. Also in 1901 a Protectorate was declared over the Northern Territories.

1912   Sir Hugh Clifford became Governor in 1912 and remained in office until 1919 after the end of World War I (1914–18). By 1912 cocoa had overtaken gold as the main export and there were prospects of a good economic future. The railway from Sekondi had reached Kumasi in 1903 and Clifford had plans for further construction, but the war put an end to these. He took charge of the expulsion of the Germans from Togoland in cooperation with the French.

1919   Brigadier General Guggisberg (later Sir Gordon Guggisberg) became Governor and Clifford became Governor of Nigeria. Guggisberg had led the surveying work in Nigeria before serving in France between 1914 and 1918. He continued plans made during Clifford's time and developed some of his own. His Governorship was marked by the completion of the railway from Accra to Kumasi, the building of Korle Bu hospital in Accra and much work on Takoradi Harbour completed after he left in 1927. He was much revered by the people of the Gold Coast whom he left with a more representative Legislative Council.

1927   Sir Ransford Slater succeeded Guggisberg. He had a difficult five years as Governor as it coincided with falling cocoa prices and the world-wide economic slump.

1932   Sir Shenton Thomas began a short period as Governor before going to Malaya, where he was Governor at the time of the Japanese invasion.

1934   Sir Arnold Hodson became Governor and continued in office until after the outbreak of war in 1939. He had to deal with cocoa hold-ups in protest against low prices. He instituted radio rediffusion in the towns.

APPENDIX II

Bibliography

ALLEN, CHARLES. *Tales from the Dark Continent*

BALFOUR, PATRICK. *Lords of the Equator*

BOXER, C. R. *The Portuguese Seaborne Empire*

BOYLE, LAURA. *Diary of a Colonial Officer's Wife*

BURNS, ALAN. *Colonial Civil Servant*

BUSIA, K. A. *The Position of the Chief in the Modern Political System of Ashanti*

CAPLAN, MARION. *The Portuguese Land and its People*

CLARIDGE, W. W. a *History of the Gold Coast and Ashanti*

COLLINS, W. B. *They Went to Bush*

COOMBS, DOUGLAS. *The Gold Coast, Britain and the Netherlands 1850–74*

DESGATE, RICHARD H. *The Conquest of Northern Nigeria*

ELLIS, A. B. *History of the Gold Coast*

FARSON, NEGLEY. *Behind God's Back*

GOLD COAST GOVERNMENT. *The Gold Coast Handbook 1937*

GREENE, GRAHAM. *The Heart of the Matter*

HAILEY, LORD. *An African Survey*

HALEY, K. H. D. *The British and the Dutch*

HUXLEY, ELSPETH. *Four Guineas*

IMRAY, COLIN. *Policeman in Africa*

KIRK-GREENE, A. H. M. *On Crown Service*
   The Corona Club, 1900–1990

LAWRENCE, A. W. *Trade, Castles and Forts of West Africa*

LEEDS, ALLEN. *Long Ago and Far Away*

MACDONALD, MALCOLM. *Bringing an End to Empire*

MASLEN, JAMES. *Beating About the Nigerian Bush*

MATSON, J. N. *Ashanti Custom*

METCALFE, G. E. *Great Britain and Ghana. Documents of Ghana History 1807–1957*
   Maclean of the Gold Coast

MULLINS, PATRICK. *Retreat from Africa*

O REGAN, JOHN. *From Empire to Commonwealth*

PACKENHAM, THOMAS *The Scramble for Africa 1876–1912*

POWELL, ERICA. *Private Secretary, Gold Coast*

RATHBONE, RICHARD *British Documents on the End of Empire* Volumes I & II, Ghana

RATTRAY, R. S. *Ashanti Law and Constitution*
   Ashanti Proverbs
   Religion and Art in Ashanti

ROONEY, DAVID. *Sir Charles Arden-Clarke*

ROYLE, TREVOR. *Winds of Change*

RUSSELL, COLIN. *Gold Coast to Ghana*

SARBAH, J. M. *Fanti Customary Laws*

THOMAS, HUGH. *The Slave Trade*

VOGT, J. *Portuguese Rule*

WARD, W. E. F. *A History of Ghana*
 My Africa

WATSON, AITKEN. *Report of the Commission of Enquiry into Disturbances in the Gold Coast*

WOLFSON, FREDA. *Pageant of Ghana*

Index

Accra, Capital of Gold Coast
5,6,9, 10, 12, 26, 31, 51, 85, 86,
99, 102, 105, 111, 140, 184, 185
Accra, Ship 145
Acolatse, Banga 128
Acolatse, Charles 128
Ada, Port 125
Ada, Ship 12, 37
Addo, Akufo 16
Adjitey, Sergeant 5
Aflao 129
Agriculture Department 21, 58
Ahanta 65, 70
Akim Abuakwa 99, 101, 173,
176, 184, 187
Akwei, Dr 120, 121
Akuse 6, 81, 106, 107
Allen, David 103
Allen, Sammy 47
Amable, Police Superintendent
140
Angola 200
Anloga 124, 130
Appleton, Oxfordshire 96
Arden-Clarke, Sir Charles 136,
152, 165, 179, 190, 197
Asafu Adjaye, Minister of Local
Government 186
Ashanti 80, 84, 90, 101, 152, 155,
179
Assembly of God 71
Atta 174, 175, 176
Aureol, Ship 193
Axim 10, 65

Ballantine, R. 102
Bannochie, Jack 122
Barringer, Terry 1, 2
Bathurst 75
Bats 66

Beeton, Hugh 53, 55, 56, 57,
156, 161, 167
Beeton, Mary 167
Belgian Congo 143, 198
Bennett, Elizabeth 92, 191, 192
Bennett, Rodney 2, 92, 185, 191,
192
Bey, Fuad 100
Blair, Robin 2, 180, 185
Blimp, Colonal 14
Bo 48
Bolagatanga 158
Bondoukou 162
Bortey, Silas 135
Bosumtwi, Lake 166
Bouert, Clayes 143
Bournemouth 59, 76
Bown, Lalage 109
Bradley, Kenneth 86
Bridport 76
British-American Tobacco
Company (BAT) 196
Britton, Lindsay 144
Brockenhurst 59
Brooks, Edgar 82, 169, 170
Brown, Maurice 126, 127
Brown, Topper 180
Buckley, (Buck) 122, 193
Buem 138
Bumpus, Bernard 191
Burden, Geoffrey 158
Burge, James 163
Burma 39, 71
Burner, Eric 61, 69
Burns, Sir Alan 53, 66, 67, 70,
79, 84, 99–102, 136

Caldow, Bill 107
Cambridge University 2, 12, 14,
35

Cansdale 96
Cape Coast 17, 18, 80, 82, 92–96, 173
Carrington, Charles 160, 161
Ceuta 8
Ceylon 6
Chadwick, E. R. 114
Chalmers, Jimmy 6
Chamberlain, Neville 14
Chitral (Ship) 40
Christiansborg Castle 5
City Hotel 49
Clark, Bob 199
Cochran, Ian 150, 173, 190
Cochran, Molly 190
Cocoa 5, 58, 62, 118
Colonial Administrative Service 7, 12
Colonial Legal Service 22
Colonial Office 13, 16
Convention Peoples Party (CPP) 101
Cooper, Roy 91, 97
Coulson, John 31
Coupland, Professor 15
Coussey, Sir Henley 103
Crawford, Jack 91, 151
Creasy, Sir Gerald 99, 101–104, 126, 136
Crofton, Pluto 28

Dafo 122
Dakar 23
Dalgleish, A. 102
Danford, Danny 92
Danquah, J. B. 6, 100, 101, 103, 173
Davies, Arthur 156, 157
Davies, Jean 157
Deakin, John 17
de Gaulle, General 23
Dekyi, Hima 66
Dennis, Faith 1, 40, 59, 60, 74, 76, 87–93, 135, 146, 147, 154, 164, 169, 171, 173
Dennis, Nigel 94, 146, 154, 164

Dennis, William 186, 187
Desirade (Ship) 60
Dickson, Alec 113, 114, 142
Dickson, John 93
Dixcove 65–67
Dixon, John 123, 130, 134, 136, 160
Dorma 161
Doz, Monsieur 128, 129
Drew, Humphrey 27
Duncan, John 187, 188
Dunkirk 34, 47
Dyk, S. 45

Earle, Dennis 176
East Africa 49, 86, 197
Education Department 21
Edusei, Krobo 167
Edwards, Gordon 161, 162
Elder Dempster 12
Elders 63
Elmina 7, 18, 109, 170
Ensor, Mike 128, 143
Ewes 124

Fairbanks, Douglas Jnr 16
Fieldgate, A. F. E. 17
Fischer, Father 88
Forbes, A. G. 188
Forestry Department 21, 172
Fortes, Professor 15
Free French Forces 31
Freetown 35–38, 41, 42
Fry, Maxwell 71
Furse, Sir Ralph 14

Gambia 26
Gandhi, Mahatma 17
Gardner, Gerry 38, 48
Gardner, Lionel 17, 23
Gass, Michael 115, 148, 154, 175
Germany 8
Ghana, Area and Location 9
Gibraltar 14, 47, 65, 108, 154
Giffard, General 31, 42
Gin, Distilled Locally 55
Gold Coast, Map 4

Gold Coast Regiment 23
Gorgori, Garuba 45
Grafton Valley 444, 45, 48
Greene, Graham 49
Gun Licences 55

Hadija, Sambo 45
Hadow, Gordon 53
Hammond, John Baffoe 68
Harding, Thomas 38
Hardy, Carol 161, 188, 189
Hardy, Donald 161, 162, 188, 189
Hardy, John 189
Harper, Frank 57
Hastwell, Ian 112
Hausa 31, 51, 52
Heaton, David 116, 141
Helps, Peter 158
Hindle, Anne 143
Hindle, Tom 106, 107, 109, 123,
    134, 141, 142
Hitler 12
Ho 107, 120, 143, 144
Hohoe 111, 112, 120, 137–139
Holland, Bishop 123, 129
HOlts, John 112
Holy Child College 88, 94
Hope, Bill 181, 182, 190, 193
Hope, Margaret 182
Horwood, Mike 82
Hurricane Aircraft 39, 48
Hyde-Clarke, Meredith 152

Ilford 40
Imray, Colin 5, 101, 102
India 6, 29, 34
Iwo 50

Japan 50
Jasikan 138
Jelacsics, Peter 126, 127
Johnson, Dr 60
Jos 35
Judd, Judy & Dot 69, 87

Kabba 82, 88, 89, 119, 134

Keatinge, Michael 41–44, 48
Kenki 24
Kerr, Alan 132
Kibi 99, 101, 173, 176, 184, 187
Kilbourn, Donald & Sheila 181,
    182, 190
Kingstone, Bob 160
Kipling 14
Kiribati 154
Koforidua 6
Korsah, Judge 183
Kpandu 105, 106, 110–123,
    136–143
Kpeve 118
Krachi 115
Kumasi 6, 89, 90, 155–161,
    166–168, 190
Kweku, Paul 134, 189

Lagos 36, 51, 92
Lane, Barry 102, 182, 183
Larkhill 27
Lawson, Stewart 173, 174, 190
Likpe Mate 137
Lilley, Captain 116, 117
Lome 124, 128, 129, 131
Loveridge 81, 83, 146, 149, 150,
    168–173
Lugard, Lord 15, 32

Mackay, Gough 17
Mackenzie, Neil 34, 46
Maclean, George 156
Macmillan, Harold 7
McMullen 166
Macpherson, Sir John 165
Magdalen College, Oxford 157
Malaria 10
Mampong 90
Mamprussi 158, 177
Mangin, Thorlief (Later Sir
    Thorlief) 15, 17, 80, 83, 84,
    90, 91, 110, 146
Matson, John 24, 155, 169, 183,
    201
Medical Department 21

Milahowski, F. 45
Milne, Malcolm 35
Mullen, (Spud) 72
Munich 14
Murray, Dr K. A. H. 102

Native Authorities Ordinance,
    1944 66
Na Yeri 158
New Northland 37
Nigeria 25, 26, 35, 38, 49, 114,
    165, 197
Nkrumah 6, 71, 101, 103, 123,
    126, 132, 144, 151, 152, 160,
    165, 188, 197
North Africa 49
Northern Territories 80, 84, 157
Nsawam 6
Nzima 132

Oda 96, 97
O'Dwyer, Pat 42
Ofori Atta, Nana Sir 99
Optimism Club 73
Oronsay (Ship) 39
Oxford University 12, 14, 35, 39,
    196
Oxford University School of
    Geography 40
Oyo 50

Padmore, G. E. 101
Pakistan 6
Palaver 43, 44, 63
Paton, Christopher 193
Patteson, Mike 172
Pepase 113
Perham, Margery 15, 16
Peters, Bill 151
Peters, Harry 127
Pith Helmets 1
Port Loko 41, 43, 44
Portuguese 7
Positive Action 144
Prempeh I, Asantehene 156
Prempeh II, Asantehene 155

Prince of Wales, HMS 41
Prison Department 19
Public Works Department 21

Quashie-Idun, Judge 160

Rattray, R. S. 201
Reed, Quartermaster 34
Repulse, HMS 41
Resident Minister 26
Rhodes House 2
Rhodesians 24
Rice-Davies, Mandy 163
Rigold, 'Driller' 130
Rombaut, Peter 198
Royal Commonwealth Society
    1, 2
Royal Geographical Society 2
Russell, Arthur 61
Russell, Colin 146, 148, 150
Russell, Jean 61

St Augustine's School 88
Saloway, Sir Reginald 105
Saltpond 91
Samaru 29
Sandemanab 158, 159
Scoles, District Magistrate, and
    wife Juliet 22
Scott, Dr David 108
Sekondi 64, 65, 71–74
Seventh Day Adventists 72
Shama 65
Sierra Leone 26, 28, 35–38, 45,
    63
Sinclair, George (Later Sir
    George) 85
Singapore 45, 47
Smith, Ambrose 90
Smith, Brian 56, 57, 69, 70,
    160, 174, 175, 186, 189, 193
Smith, Margaret 57, 175, 193
Spicer, John 17
Spooner, Arthur 89
Stanleyville 198, 199
Stevenson, D. 97

Sunyani 157
Swayne, Christopher 46

Tachie-Menson 71
Takoradi 51, 53, 61, 75
Tantum 82
Tarkwa 17, 51, 53, 57, 58
Togbe Sri 130
Togoland 8, 105–123, 136–144,
    159, 167, 179
Togo Union 108, 109
Townsend, Suzanne 97, 145
Townsend, Tony 97, 145
Tristram, Dale 72

U. Boats 27, 37
United Gold Coast Convention
    (UGCC) 101
United Nations 9
Urwick Orr 168

Van Gaskell, Father 123
Van lare, Willy 159
Vichy 23, 31
Volta River 23, 123, 124

Walker, Richard 105, 106

Wallace, Reg 153, 154
Wardzala, Jan 113
Wassaw 56
Watson, Aitken 5, 6, 101–103
Watson, Dickie 47
Weatherburn, Morton 137, 141
Wemagah 168
West Africa Court of Appeal 26
Westwood, Deryck 115, 118, 119
Westwood, Margot 118, 119
White, Mrs Eirene 167
Wiawso 61
Wilberforce Camp 38
Wimshurst, Hugh 65
Winneba 140
Wolseley, Sir Garnet 156
Woolley, Ron 192
Woolner, General 38, 42, 45
Woolwich 40, 42
Worawora 115

Yau 88
Young, A. E. 167

Zaria 25, 26, 28, 29, 32
Zuru Audu 36